Journey TO
SIGNIFICANCE

Other Books by Kimberly Sowell

Journey to Confidence: Becoming Women Who Witness

A Month of Miracles: 30 Stories of the Unmistakable Presence of God
Coauthored with other Women by Design authors

Journey TO SIGNIFICANCE

BECOMING WOMEN *of* DIVINE DESTINY

KIMBERLY SOWELL

NEW HOPE
PUBLISHERS

Birmingham, Alabama

New Hope® Publishers
P. O. Box 12065
Birmingham, AL 35202-2065
www.newhopepublishers.com

New Hope Publishers is a division of WMU®.

Library of Congress Cataloging-in-Publication Data

Sowell, Kimberly.
  Journey to significance : becoming women of divine destiny / Kimberly Sowell.
    p. cm.
  ISBN 978-1-59669-217-6 (sc)
  1. Christian women--Religious life--Biblical teaching. 2. Christian life--Biblical teaching. I. Title.
  BV4527.S649 2008
  248.8'43--dc22

                    2008007402

Cover Design: Left Coast Design, lcoast.com

ISBN-10: 1-59669-217-0
ISBN-13: 978-1-59669-217-6

N084140 • 0808 • 3M1

With great love and appreciation to my family.
You have enriched my walk on my journey
to significance.

Table *of* Contents

Preface

How to Use This Book

Journey to Significance may be studied as an individual or as a group Bible study. Each chapter contains exercises to help you learn and apply each concept. Watch for these symbols:

Focus on You: Opening personal-reflection question to help you evaluate how you currently relate to the chapter's topic. Warning: You do not want to skim over this question! Set the tone for reading the chapter by opening your heart for an honest evaluation of your personal thoughts and feelings.

Stepping-Stone: Study questions sprinkled throughout the body of the chapter. Stepping-Stones will help you stay on track with the message and reinforce the Scripture of the chapter.

Retracing Your Steps to Stay on Course: Closing personal response guide to help you embrace the "life lesson" and "significance connection" of each chapter. As the Word of God penetrates your heart, the Holy Spirit will begin to change your attitudes and strengthen your mind. Allow God to guide you in your answers to these questions.

Stepping Up to the Challenge: Practical application exercise. God imparts His wisdom and knowledge into our lives to change our thinking as well as our actions. God can change your life through this Bible study, but only if you put it into practice, applying His truth in your actions.

Introduction

Significance. It's not really a "feel good" word for happy thoughts and restful moments. It's a sobering word, one that requires serious reflection and personal evaluation. This single word represents the stuff that we're all searching for in our lives. We don't want simply to exist; we want to thrive.

Journey to Significance is an interactive Bible study to help women who are searching for significance. Life is indeed a journey, not a destination. God is going before us to carve a path of abundant joy, powerful influence, challenging vision, sweet fellowship, and spiritual satisfaction, and how we respond to God's will today affects our ability to fulfill God's purpose for tomorrow.

As we enjoy getting to know six men and women from Scripture, we're going to study the breath-taking significance of decisions they made along their journeys. Each character had a significant destiny in the kingdom of God, but it was their *daily decisions* that determined their ability to successfully fulfill God's specific purpose for their lives. Each of their days was filled with significance, not just some singular moment in time when they reached a particular marker of success, because each day afforded them opportunities to build the kingdom of God.

What about you? Each day, your life can be significant if you are fulfilling God's purpose—if you are seeking first the kingdom of God (Matthew 6:33). Your today is filled with God's opportunities for you to grow your spiritual character. Today is filled with opportunities to glorify God and grow His kingdom. You will find your greatest fulfillment in life when you embrace this truth: your journey to significance is not about *you* being important, but it's about you fulfilling God's very significant plan for His very significant purpose—to draw all people unto Himself (John 12:32). He wants to accomplish that purpose through His plan for you.

I encourage you to recruit a prayer advocate while you complete this study. As you determine in your heart to fulfill God's great purpose for your life, you can be sure that the enemy (I won't even give him the pleasure of getting his name on the page!) will throw confusion and doubt at your heart. As he shoots those fiery darts at you, hold up your shield of faith. Bundle up those lies with your belt of truth, and send them to the throne room of God, marked: "Please do not return to sender!" (See Ephesians 6:14–17.)

God is faithful, and He will guard your heart and mind if you ask Him for guidance and discernment.

I pray that many godly women will find the significance and purpose they are seeking through this Bible study. May blessings, growth spurts, joyful tears, and belly laughs mark your journey!

There are many plans in a man's heart, nevertheless, the LORD's *counsel—that will stand.*
—Proverbs 19:21

1

Joseph, Son of Jacob

Taking the Scenic Route: Building Character Through Perseverance

LIFE LESSON OF JOSEPH: Through his continued faithfulness to God, Joseph was a witness for the one true living God.

SIGNIFICANCE CONNECTION: God gives every believer a vision of His desired future for his or her life; along with the ups and downs of the spiritual journey are several opportunities to use one's hardships to testify of God's faithfulness.

My little girl carefully rests her gaudy plastic tiara squarely over her ears, twirls gracefully (until she runs into the refrigerator), and announces that she is going to be a princess ballerina when she grows up. Fascinating! But the next day, as she removes giant pretend splinters from her dolly's belly button while taking Mr. Bear's temperature with the toy thermometer jammed between his toes, she decides that her destiny is to be a pediatrician. No problem! Never mind that she will have to find and marry a prince and take years of dancing lessons to find a poise she could not inherit from her momma, *or* excel in math and science classes at a respectable university and work her way through med school in order to fulfill her dreams. She doesn't look worried about accomplishing either goal. She states her future profession with certainty and a smile. Why not? She's six. She's not concerned about the road trip; she is focused on the destination.

The dreams of children are made of hope and imagination, with little more. They view life with a gigantic blind spot for limitations. We adults would chase a dream with the same reckless abandon had it not been for the numerous disappointments and failures we've experienced on former road trips, chasing passions of the heart. But, what if the dream is of God? What do you do when God whispers a destination in your ear?

 Focus on You

Commit a quiet moment prayerfully to search your heart. What is the pursuit or the dream God has planted in your heart? Ask God to confirm that this pursuit is from Him. If you can't find a vision, ask God to prepare you for availability to answer His calling, and begin listening daily with an open heart.

Enter into a time of prayer, asking God to help you learn a life lesson from Joseph and to make the significance connection within your own life.

What to Do with a Vision
Read Genesis 37:1–11 in your Bible.

Joseph was a young man with a big dream. At 17, he had lived a sheltered life in a loving, albeit dysfunctional family. Joseph was the eleventh of 12 sons, and firstborn to his mother, Rachel, the cherished sweetheart wife of his father, Jacob. Rachel later died during the childbirth of her second son, Jacob's twelfth and last, Benjamin. As Jacob looked in the eyes of Joseph, surely he saw the eyes of his beloved Rachel, endearing Joseph to his father's heart. Jacob favored Joseph above his other sons and made this fact abundantly clear as he bestowed upon Joseph a prized "*coat of many colors*" (KJV).

With "favorite son" status, Joseph's brothers "*hated him and could not speak peaceably to him*" (Genesis 37:4). Despite their hatred, Joseph nurtured an abundance of self-esteem and didn't appear surprised when he received through two dreams a vision of future glory. Joseph first dreamed he and his brothers were binding sheaves in the field, when suddenly his sheaf arose to stand erect while the other sheaves bowed to his sheaf. His second dream was of the sun, moon, and 11 stars bowing to him.

Stepping-Stone

Read Genesis 37:5–8 again.
1. What did Joseph do after his first dream experience?

2. The Hebrew word for "bow" found in verse 7 indicates paying homage to royalty or to God. How did his brothers respond to this notion?

3. Read Genesis 37:9–11 again. Based on his brothers' reaction to the first dream, what do you suppose was Joseph's motivation for telling them about his second dream?

Consider what Joseph did *not* do after having these visions of reigning power. He apparently did not carefully ponder the dreams in his heart before sharing them with his family. He did not seek his father's advice or consult with anyone for spiritual guidance. We see no evidence that Joseph prayed to the Lord for clarification, confirmation, to say a word of praise or thanks, or even to ask the Lord to prepare him for such an awesome responsibility. He appears to have accepted the dreams with an overconfident spirit. Did he think he deserved such respect from his family, even his own father, to bow before him?

Joseph had known few hardships. He was spiritually young-minded; he was relishing in his future splendors without giving thought to the awesome responsibility of being placed in leadership by the hand of the Lord. Little did Joseph know that his envisioned royal position was not to be for his glory, but for the welfare of a whole nation.

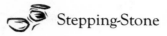 Stepping-Stone

Read Proverbs 13:10 and Proverbs 28:25 in the margin and respond to the questions below.

By pride comes nothing but strife, but with the well-advised is wisdom.
—Proverbs 13:10

He who is of a proud heart stirs up strife, but he who trusts in the Lord will be prospered.
—Proverbs 28:25

"For whoever exalts himself will be humbled, and he who humbles himself will be exalted."
—Luke 14:11

Then they said to one another, "Look, this dreamer is coming!"
—Genesis 37:19

1. Joseph took the dreams God had given him, and his communication stirred up strife amongst his family. They could not rejoice with him at this good news because they presumably sensed the pride in Joseph's heart, leaving them even angrier and more jealous. Have you ever faced strife with your peers as a result of receiving an honor? How could pride on your part have aggravated the ill feelings of others?

2. According to Proverbs 28:25, what is a difference between the proud and those who trust God? (Read Luke 14:11 for further insight.)

A humble spirit doesn't require us to stumble over our personal shortcomings. Remember that God grew impatient with Moses for his many excuses when God called him to go before Pharaoh (Exodus 4:1-14). However, a humble spirit acknowledges that all blessings and honors come from the Lord, and that we must rely on the Lord for strength and wisdom. A humble spirit realizes the gravity of fulfilling our responsibilities with excellence to glorify God and bless others. A humble spirit is aware that God-given privileges are not merely for our enjoyment but also for the growth and welfare of the kingdom of God.

Are we there yet?
Read Genesis 37:12–36 in your Bible.
Joseph's brothers had not forgotten about Joseph's prophetic dreams. In fact, his dreams must have climbed to the top of their list of reasons why they hated Joseph, because they had nicknamed him the "dreamer" (Genesis 37:19).

Whether they believed the dreams were from God or not, Joseph's brothers desired to thwart any chances for Joseph to rise to success. After deciding against killing him, they sold him into slavery.

As Joseph watched in disbelief the transaction that sold his life away for 20 shekels of silver and was hauled away in bondage, what a flood of emotions and bewilderment might have crowded out hope in his heart. What now of the visions of greatness? How could there be any hope that anyone would ever bow to him now? His life was worthless, stolen from him by his hate-filled brothers. Or was it?

Consider this common disconnect of faith that creates unnecessary despair in many believers' hearts. Do you believe God has a plan for your life and that His desire is for your good (Jeremiah 29:11–13)? I pray you are saying yes with all of your heart! Then why would you despair when someone or something comes along and harms you? Can any person—an unfair boss, a disbelieving spouse, a terrorist, or anybody—thwart God's will? Is there any force of nature, including a tornado or hurricane or eathquake, out of God's control?

When trials and loss come your way, you can trust that God is never sitting on His throne, taken aback by the event that has just taken place, for God is in control whether the climate is balmy or stormy. "No weapon formed against you shall prosper" (Isaiah 54:17) to overturn the will of God. You may not have seen it coming, but God did.

Reuben, as firstborn, probably had the greatest reason to dislike Joseph. After all, as the oldest son, he should have had the honor of "favorite son" status, and if any son would be leader over the family, the lot likely would have fallen to him by family custom. However, it was Reuben who first kept his brothers from murdering Joseph and who concocted the plot to throw him in the pit so he could later return Joseph home unharmed. Reuben's ultimate plan was to help Joseph, but Reuben's intended plan was not God's plan. God's will prevailed.

If you already know the full story of Joseph's rise to power, you know that it was necessary for Joseph to make his way to Egypt and take up various roles that would strengthen his soul, build his faith, and teach him about living for God in that pagan culture. Sometimes the disappointments of our lives, when we thought someone was going to help us reach new heights or improve our situation yet it didn't happen, are actually God's hand of denial because He's reserving an even greater blessing for just the right time. The easy way out is not always God's way out.

For I know the thoughts that I think toward you, says the LORD, thoughts of peace and not of evil, to give you a future and a hope. Then you will call upon Me and go and pray to Me, and I will listen to you. And you will seek Me and find Me, when you search for Me with all your heart.
—Jeremiah 29:11–13

In Joseph's bewildered, jumbled thoughts on the road to Egypt, I wonder if the idea occurred to him that God would still fulfill the dreams of reigning power. I also wonder if Joseph realized God would use this leg of his life journey to prepare him for leadership.

When God gives us a glimpse of a bright spot in the future, when do we want it to happen? Now! Who needs to prepare? Let's get to the good stuff! Our prayer lives can sound like the redundant chorus of children in the back seat: *are we there yet? Are we there yet?* So many times in my own life, I thought I was ready to step into a role, only to find that I was sorely unprepared. God usually hasn't taken the most direct route to get me from point A to point B in my journey to significance, but instead has taken me along the scenic route, to give me the extra time needed to grow spiritually. As a young man, Joseph still had much to learn about the world, about leadership, about himself, and most of all, about the faithfulness of God. God would prove His faithfulness to Joseph, for Joseph was being prepared by God to be a leader and an agent of hope in some very bleak days ahead for the people of Egypt.

Stepping-Stone

1. Fill in the blanks of Proverbs 29:25.
   The fear of _____ brings a _____, but whoever trusts in the _____ shall be _____.

2. Can you think of a figure in the Bible who feared men's actions so much that he faltered?

3. When you think about someone "robbing" you of God's blessings, what is your greatest fear? How do you act on that fear?

4. As Joseph was hauled away in bondage, two significant questions may have arisen in his mind: *were the dreams just in my imagination, born out of wishful thinking?* And, *does God go with me as I'm traveling to Egypt to be a slave?* Precious sister, hardships are not a measurement of God's favor. You may be exactly on the right course and facing hardships daily, or completely off course and feeling no consequences at the moment. Meditate on the words of God: *"I will not leave you nor forsake you"* (Joshua 1:5). Apply His promise to your current discouragements, writing your thoughts below.

But in Everything Give Thanks

With three very small children, our most quoted Bible verse in our home is 1 Thessalonians 5:18: *"In everything give thanks; for this is the will of God in Christ Jesus for you."* If you don't care for the green beans on your plate tonight, you can be grateful they aren't Brussels sprouts. Though you're disappointed about the rainy day, be glad the plants and animals are receiving a drink. While you don't understand why you can't wear pink *every* day, be glad that you have clean clothes to wear. I have tried to insist upon myself that I also apply this verse to every disappointment in my life, but when my heart is broken and I am disillusioned beyond my ability to see any blessings in my despair, I can praise God and give thanks that He who calls me is faithful, who also will do it (1 Thessalonians 5:24).

He who calls you is faithful, who also will do it.
—1 Thessalonians 5:24

Note two great symbols in this pivotal moment of Joseph's life. Joseph's brothers stripped him of his coat of many colors, symbolically stripping him of his family status and dignity. However, their father Jacob's love and favor could never be stripped from Joseph by the hands of his brothers. People who seek to harm you or who are willing to step on your back to improve their lot may desire to strip you of your dignity, to make you feel little and worthless, especially as a Christian. However, they are unable to separate you from your Heavenly Father's love and favor, and they cannot deny you the dignity and status that comes with being a daughter in the family of God. Praise God and give thanks for that!

The pit also creates a poignant symbol. Imagine the clawing and begging that may have come from Joseph as he panicked in that dark narrow pit. (We learn in Genesis 42:21 that Joseph pled for his life from the pit, the first of

And we know that all things work together for good to those who love God, to those who are the called according to His purpose.
—Romans 8:28

My enemies without cause hunted me down like a bird. They silenced my life in the pit and threw stones at me. The waters flowed over my head; I said, "I am cut off!" I called on Your name, O LORD, from the lowest pit. You have heard my voice: "Do not hide Your ear from my sighing, from my cry for help." You drew near on the day I called on You, and said, "Do not fear!" O Lord, You have pleaded the case for my soul; You have redeemed my life.
—Lamentations 3:52–58

many humbling experiences for Joseph.) That pit could be either a place of life-giving water, or a place of burial and imprisonment; this event of being sold into slavery served as both in Joseph's life—it was life-giving in that he was spared being murdered by his brothers and was being set on a path for greatness in Egypt, while also being that temporary cell of imprisonment. When we find ourselves in a pit, we can give thanks because God is working all things together for the good of those who love Him and are called according to His purpose (Romans 8:28).

 Stepping-Stone

1. Ecclesiastes. 10:8 says, *"He who digs a pit will fall into it."* His brothers forsook Joseph, but their evil plot would eventually come back around to them. Have you ever sinned against someone, only to have the shame fall back on you?

2. Read Lamentations 3:52–58.

    •   What is your first reaction when you feel under attack?

    •   In verse 57, what is God's first response?

    •   As you examine verse 58, think about the depths of God's rescue efforts for you.

3. When an unexpected trial arises in your life, your response indicates to others how much or little you trust God. Your response is your testimony. Think about the unbelievers in your sphere of influence who watch you

carefully because of your faith. What response to crisis testifies to the faithfulness of God?

4. God loved Joseph and knew every detail of the injustice he was suffering; yet, note that God didn't step in and rescue him. Ask God to help you determine why, and write your thoughts below.

A Stop Along the Way
Read Genesis 39:1–20 in your Bible.
Joseph was sold in Egypt to Potiphar, an officer of Pharaoh and captain of the guard. Joseph had the Lord as His guide, and Joseph prospered (v. 2), which might be roughly rendered "he went through." Joseph's ability to prosper was not limited by his location or station in life, but it had everything to do with the Lord's hand upon him. He was willing to go forward, to "go through" what was set before him. Joseph never could have enjoyed success in Potiphar's house had he chosen to be filled with anger and resentment. Instead of passing the time dwelling on the past, mourning what might have been, or plotting escape and revenge, Joseph made the choice to be at peace as he trusted God's plan.

Potiphar took note of Joseph. In verse 3, Potiphar didn't simply think of Joseph as talented or capable; somehow Potiphar was able to perceive that God was bringing success into Joseph's life. Now *that* was the biggest success of Joseph's stay in Potiphar's home—through his faithfulness, he was a witness for God! Potiphar was highly blessed of God for Joseph's sake (v. 5).

 Stepping-Stone

Consider your productivity and work ethic in your home, church, and community. Which statement best matches how others would describe you?

- ❏ She makes effort to be recognized and rewarded for her work.
- ❏ She lives for the weekend; fun and leisure are what she values most.
- ❏ When the cat's away, that mouse is at play!
- ❏ She complains a lot.
- ❏ She is a joy to be around, and she helps me do the best I can at my work.
- ❏ She gives her best in everything she does, like she is doing it to please God.
- ❏ God has His hand on her life, and she lets Him shine through in everything she does.

The Temptation to Settle

Proverbs 10:6 teaches, *"Blessings are on the head of the righteous."* Joseph's commitment to righteousness was put to the test through the invitations of Potiphar's wife. Joseph was tempted daily to succumb to Potiphar's wife, and surely some days he felt stronger than others, yet he remained faithful to his master and to his God.

On the day of the accused rape attempt, the elements were in place for a perfect storm. Joseph was all alone with her, having no witness to corroborate his defense. Potiphar's wife had misleading evidence: his garment in her hands. Joseph had motive, being a single man with the opportunity to satisfy his flesh while also disgracing his master. And last, there couldn't have been a more credible witness to Potiphar than his very own wife. By all appearances, things couldn't have gone worse for Joseph. However, once again God was using an injustice against Joseph for his good; without the deceitful accusations of Potiphar's wife, Potiphar may never have been willing to release the hard-working Joseph from his household, and Joseph would have remained in bondage.

What a great temptation we all face to settle for less than God's best. If Joseph had been a lesser man, he might have weighed the situation carefully and decided he could be content as a chief slave having a regular affair with his boss's wife. It would have been a pitiful waste if Joseph had taken a lesser route, robbing himself of God's best. He would have dishonored God, ruined his witness to everyone in Potiphar's household, and potentially destroyed his future as a mighty leader in Egypt. His sin eventually would have caught up with him, bringing terrible consequences for his actions.

 Stepping-Stone

1. Fill in the blanks below for Psalm 1:1–3 (NKJV):

    Blessed is the man who walks not in the counsel of the _____,
    nor stands in the _____*, nor sits in the seat of the* _____*;
    but his delight is in the _____*, and in His law he*
    _____ *day and night. He shall be like*
    a _____ *planted by the rivers of water, that brings forth its fruit*
    _____*, whose leaf also shall not* _____*; and*
    whatever he does shall _____*.*

    What does Psalm 1:1–3 teach you about your journey to significance?

2. You're on a road bound for greatness for God's kingdom, but like Joseph, you first might have to experience some trials and difficulties. What may seem like delays are actually interventions of God on your journey to significance, but these delays, these times of "holding patterns" as you wait on God to move, can be a great temptation just to pitch a tent, build a fence, and settle in permanently! Friend, if you choose to stall out where God tells you to wait, you're settling for less than God's best. Enter into a time of prayer, and listen carefully for God's voice. Ask God to show you any areas of your life where you are doing any of the following:
    *   giving into temptations and damaging your witness for Christ
    *   settling in where God instead wants you to move on, thus delaying your progress in the Lord
    *   thinking too small for what God has in store for your life

Under Attack

Joseph's brothers attacked Joseph personally because he had something they wanted, and Potiphar's wife was no different. As Christians, we also can expect to be attacked because we have what others want: peace, joy, love, hope, and all of the other marks of God's favor that rest upon a believer. The Apostle Peter wrote, *"Beloved, do not think it strange concerning the fiery trial which is to try you, as though some strange thing happened to you; but rejoice to the extent that you partake of Christ's sufferings"* (1 Peter. 4:12–13). Your willingness to endure personal attacks will not be in vain, as God will use your quiet assurance as a testimony of His great power.

When Visible Doors Don't Open
Read Genesis 39:21 through 41:16 in your Bible.

When Joseph went to prison, he began the third leg of his journey to significance. As Joseph interpreted the dream of the chief butler that foretold he was returning to Pharaoh, Joseph must have started packing his bags. *Oh, boy! This is it! I'm getting out of this prison, and my dream from God is going to come true!* In his dysfunctional home, perhaps Joseph assumed that one day his father would have the connections to get him into leadership for his dream to be fulfilled. When Joseph landed in Potiphar's house, maybe the thought crossed his mind that God would somehow allow him to connect with some dignitary who entered Potiphar's home. Neither connection created the open door for Joseph. But now, he had a connection to Pharaoh himself through his chief butler. As the chief butler's name was called through the prison's portals, and he ascended the stairs to his freedom, Joseph's heart must have leapt for joy. It was only a matter of time.

Yes, it was a matter of quite a bit of time, because *"the chief butler did not remember Joseph, but forgot him"* (Genesis 40:23). The unbelieving butler was made a free man, but the faithful Joseph had to wait another two years before God brought Joseph before the throne of Pharaoh.

 Stepping-Stone

1. Put yourself in Joseph's sandals. What thoughts would have run through your mind during those three days leading to the release of the butler?

2. How many days would have passed after the butler's release before you would have been tempted to give up hope? Have you ever felt like the world has left you behind? What prompted those thoughts?

3. Was there a purpose for the remaining two years when Joseph stayed in prison? Were they two years wasted? Read Psalm 18:16–19 and respond.

4. Joseph may have been one of those amazing figures of Scripture who never doubted God, or he may have had a few dark days during those two years after the butler's release. You and I can only imagine how difficult it is for an unbeliever to face trials and seemingly hopeless situations. What can you say to an unbeliever to encourage her to trust God in difficult times? Respond to these verses concerning the ways of God.

He sent from above, He took me; He drew me out of many waters. He delivered me from my strong enemy, from those who hated me, for they were too strong for me. They confronted me in the day of my calamity, but the LORD was my support. He also brought me out into a broad place; He delivered me because He delighted in me.
—Psalm 18:16–19

"For My thoughts are not your thoughts, nor are your ways My ways," says the LORD. *"For as the heavens are higher than the earth, so are My ways higher than your ways, and My thoughts than your thoughts."*
—Isaiah 55:8–9

As for God, His way is perfect; the word of the LORD *is proven; He is a shield to all who trust in Him.*
—Psalm 18:30

Who is wise? Let him understand these things. Who is prudent? Let him know them. For the ways of the LORD *are right; the righteous walk in them, but transgressors stumble in them.*
—Hosea 14:9

Oh, the depth of the riches both of the wisdom and knowledge of God! How unsearchable are His judgments and His ways past finding out! "For who has known the mind of the LORD? *Or who has become His counselor? Or who has first given to Him and it shall be repaid to him?" For of Him and through Him and to Him are all things, to whom be glory forever. Amen.*
—Romans 11:33–36

Commit at least one of these passages to memory to share with unbelievers when they confide in you about their heartaches. If you have an unbelieving friend who is struggling right now, send her a card or an email with one of these verses attached.

Fully Prepared, Fully Restored
Read Genesis 41:17–57 in your Bible.

By this stage in Joseph's life, he had matured. God had assured Joseph He was continuing to favor him, allowing Joseph to prosper as a slave and now as a prisoner. His new stations in life had humbled Joseph, and he had learned to appreciate the value of favor. Joseph spoke of God before interpreting the dreams for the butler and baker, and the same Joseph who once was quick to set forth his visions of greatness now exercised discretion, not seizing the opportunity to tell the two men about his dream from God at age seventeen. Joseph had learned from experience to wait upon the Lord in faith during the bleakest of circumstances. And now, Joseph's mature self-discipline guided his words before Pharaoh—not boasting, not self-seeking, not panicked or starstruck. As he finally had the opportunity to stand before a man who could make his dreams come true, he made no attempt to "seize the brass ring." Instead, Joseph took the golden opportunity to bring glory to God: *"It is not in me; God will give Pharaoh an answer of peace"* (Genesis 41:16).

"It is not in me; God will give Pharaoh an answer of peace."
—Genesis 41:16b

Joseph's tribulations had produced within him perseverance, and his perseverance had built character, and the character had birthed a lasting hope in his heart that did not disappoint (Romans 5:3–5). In one unexpected yet long-awaited night, God fulfilled the final step to place Joseph in authority. Much trial had brought much wisdom to one so young, as Joseph was just 30 years old on that amazing night when Pharaoh promoted him to authority. Joseph had been perfectly prepared to be second in command, for he had held that position in Jacob's home, at Potiphar's house, in prison, and finally in all of Egypt. He once was stripped of the honorable robe from his father, a coat of many colors, but God restored the honorable robe to Joseph in a manner of greater value. What is taken from us because human sources despise us for God's sake, God will restore in His glorious ways, either on earth or in heaven.

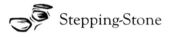 Stepping-Stone

1. Consider the names Joseph gave his sons (Genesis 41:51–52). Their names indicated that Joseph's heart was healed. Have you suffered loss? It's time for you to move forward with healing.

   - Joseph's firstborn was named to proclaim that God had helped him forget all he had suffered as well as all he had been made to leave behind. Write below all you have suffered and what you have left behind for Christ's sake. Do you need to talk to God about these life experiences? Keep talking with him until you can declare in truth, "God has made me forget."

   - The name of Joseph's second child proclaimed how God had made Joseph fruitful in the land of his affliction. Dear friend, do you need to take a step of faith to witness to someone or a group of people, knowing that taking that step will possibly bring you into the land of affliction? Answer this question after a careful search of your heart: do you trust God to make you fruitful if you step into that land of affliction?

2. Joseph was bound for a powerful position, and God first prepared him to be humble. Do you have a personal experience of being humbled? How does godly humility make you a more effective witness for Christ?

> *Joseph called the name of the firstborn Manasseh: "For God has made me forget all my toil and all my father's house." And the name of the second he called Ephraim: "For God has caused me to be fruitful in the land of my affliction."*
> —Genesis 41:51–52

3. Paul wrote that his conversion took place *"when it pleased God"* (Galatians 1:15). Once again, God's timing is perfect, but we cannot comprehend God's ways. Paul was converted after being responsible for much suffering and persecution of the early Christians. Instead of letting his past failure ruin his ability for future success, Paul was able to "go through," to prosper. Have you let go of your past failures in order to prosper in the work of the kingdom of God?

But Now

Read Genesis 42–45 in your Bible.

These four chapters of Scripture are high drama! (If you skimmed through these chapters, don't cheat yourself—go back and read them again!) As the seven years of plenty ended and famine set in (Genesis 41:53–57), the story fast forwards like a movie, advancing to 22 years after Joseph first dreamed of ruling. For 22 years, Joseph had been growing and learning in his walk with God. For 22 years, Jacob continued to mourn the loss of Joseph and had transferred his preferential treatment to Benjamin. And for 22 years, the other 10 brothers of Joseph had suffered the weight of heavy guilt. When Joseph began to interrogate them, their first thought was of their sin against their brother many years ago. They had spent 22 years looking over their shoulders, waiting for their sins to catch up with them.

Joseph, on the other hand, had chosen not to look back. When he revealed his identity to his brothers, Joseph said he was the one they had sold into slavery, and then he said, *"But now..."* (Genesis 45:5a; emphasis mine). As you suffer troubles on your journey to significance, hold fast to God, resting in the assurance that "but now" moments are coming! Perspective is sweet nectar on the other side of despair, as you feel those words roll off your tongue: "but now...." We will learn time and time again during this Bible study that those who have gone before us on a journey to significance eventually reached a spiritual marker in their lives when they got beyond what they were feeling and experiencing personally, to realize the golden piece of information: *it's not about me.* Joseph didn't gloat before his brothers, nor did he frame his success as God's favoritism as he might have done as a young man. Instead, Joseph was able to be a living witness for God before them. Joseph told his brothers that God had preserved his life that he might preserve the lives of others (Genesis 45:5, 7).

One of the most difficult trials of my life has been my battle with infertility. Many times I cried out to God, "Why me? Why did you single me out to have these problems? Why can't I have a child?" Eventually God did open my womb and I gave birth to a baby girl, praise God, but my medical problems that caused the infertility immediately ensued after her birth. When my husband and I decided we wanted another child, we chose to adopt a son, a step we probably wouldn't have taken if my medical problems had gone away.

On the other side of that battle with infertility, I can see now what was happening: God had no problem allowing me to deal with that trial in order to deliver that abandoned little boy out of hopelessness and into our home. And of course, I have also been blessed beyond measure because of our adopted son and the love he has brought into our home. But I also don't take lightly the spiritual blessings I received by walking the valley of infertility. I learned to trust God even in a situation that was totally out of my control: the health of my body. I have a "but now" testimony. God had positioned me to bless another person, my little son Jay, but I was blessed in the process as well.

 Stepping-Stone

It's too significant to miss, so I ask you to follow Joseph's example and please say this statement aloud: **God has preserved my life that I might preserve the lives of others.** Read Matthew 28:18–20. What is your role in preserving the lives of others? Are you fulfilling that role?

And Jesus came and spoke to them, saying, "All authority has been given to Me in heaven and on earth. Go therefore and make disciples of all the nations, baptizing them in the name of the Father and of the Son and of the Holy Spirit, teaching them to observe all things that I have commanded you; and lo, I am with you always, even to the end of the age." Amen.
—Matthew 28:18–20

Why Forgiveness Makes Sense

If you've ever suffered an injustice at someone else's hand, you know that Joseph wasn't able to forgive his brothers simply because he had landed in such a great station in life. No, bitter unforgiveness will take up residence in the souls of rich and poor alike. Blaming was no longer important to Joseph because he fully believed God had been in control of his journey every step of the way. Joseph told his brothers, *"So now it was not you who sent me here, but*

Joseph said to them, "Do not be afraid, for am I in the place of God? But as for you, you meant evil against me; but God meant it for good, in order to bring it about as it is this day, to save many people alive."
—Genesis 50:19–20

God" (Genesis 45:8). Even in their crime of passion, seizing an unplanned opportunity to destroy Joseph's future, they were only playing a role under the orchestration of God's master plan. Praise our all-knowing, all-powerful God! Nothing and no one, in the heavenly realm or here on earth, will thwart God's plans for your future. What is yours by God's intentions, no one can take from you. And what is not in His perfect will, you don't want anyway, no matter how shiny and glamorous it seems, because God's plan is *always* best.

Embracing this reality will make it much easier for you to forgive someone who has wronged you. Joseph also said to his brothers, *"But as for you, you meant evil against me; but God meant it for good"* (Genesis 50:20a). You can forgive others, knowing that God allowed the wrongdoing to happen for your ultimate good, if you only will allow God to teach you that lesson and bring you to new heights. And even when you haven't yet received the "good" God has intended for you, like Joseph, you must fight the temptation to take vengeance, because only Holy God is judge (Genesis 50:19). Just as God has extended grace to you over and over again, God loves your enemy and is willing to extend grace to that person as He draws him or her into a saving knowledge of Jesus Christ.

 Stepping-Stone

1. Which option best describes your approach toward those who have wronged you?

   ❑ When people hurt me, I don't deal with the pain, and I try to avoid being hurt again.

   ❑ I often try to act like what they did to me didn't bother me, but the hurt gets buried inside.

   ❑ I daydream about revenge, though I wouldn't go through with those plans.

   ❑ I retaliate quickly and get the anger out.

   ❑ I pray for God's help to forgive them.

Journey to SIGNIFICANCE

2. Think now about someone who has recently wronged you. If given the opportunity to minister in the name of Jesus to that person today, could you do it?

☐ No, I was too ungodly in the way I responded to her, and she wouldn't think I was being sincere.

☐ No, I cut off all meaningful contact with that person in order to protect myself, and I don't know if I want to help him in any way.

☐ No, I am too hurt/too angry to let God's love flow through me.

☐ Yes, I have forgiven her, and I want to love her as Jesus loves her.

3. Read Ephesians 4:32 and Colossians 3:13. What do these two verses have in common as they instruct us on how to forgive others?

And be kind to one another, tenderhearted, forgiving one another, even as God in Christ forgave you.
—Ephesians 4:32

Bearing with one another, and forgiving one another, if anyone has a complaint against another; even as Christ forgave you, so you also must do.
—Colossians 3:13

My dad has been a great sounding board for me as I have traversed many a stormy path. For all of the many times I have come to him for guidance, he always has responded to me in love, but he never has indulged me in self-pity. Instead, he has instructed me to approach every problem in life as an opportunity to build godly character. Dear friend, your life is going to be marked with one character-building opportunity after another. How you will respond to trials is significant to your journey, for the journey isn't just about you; people are watching you and will learn about the trustworthiness of God as you count Him trustworthy. Persevere.

Therefore, having been justified by faith, we have peace with God through our Lord Jesus Christ, through whom also we have access by faith into this grace in which we stand, and rejoice in hope of the glory of God. And not only that, but we also glory in tribulations, knowing that tribulation produces perseverance; and perseverance, character; and character, hope. Now hope does not disappoint, because the love of God has been poured out in our hearts by the Holy Spirit who was given to us.
—Romans 5:1–5

Retracing Your Steps to Stay on Course

LIFE LESSON OF JOSEPH: Through his continued faithfulness to God, Joseph was a witness for the one true living God.

I want my life to be significant for the Lord. I understand that life is a journey with many opportunities to grow, and I desire consistent faithfulness to God. I fully believe God has a great plan for my life. I will choose to endure hardships and prosper in God's hands despite my circumstances, because my hope comes from God. I am releasing the following circumstances to God, and I will not allow these temporary hardships to weaken my resolve to move forward for Christ.

I choose to prosper in my walk with Christ despite these circumstances:

1.

2.

3.

4.

SIGNIFICANCE CONNECTION: God gives every believer a vision of His desired future for his or her life; along the ups and downs of the spiritual journey are several opportunities to use one's hardships to testify of the faithfulness of God.

As God gives me clarity about His direction for my life, I will not lose sight of the fact that my purpose is to glorify God and bring others to Jesus. I refuse to let my hardships be in vain, for they are tremendous, God-ordained opportunities for me to testify of the faithfulness of God to the world. As I approach the following trials in my life, I am going to make some adjustments as God leads me to better reflect Christ's glory to others.

THE TRIAL I'M FACING	HOW I'M GOING TO REFLECT CHRIST'S GLORY
1.	
2.	
3.	

Stepping Up to the Challenge

Hindsight yields great perspective. I can reflect on how God has intervened in my difficult trials to bless me, often despite my lack of faith. Though I praise God that I came through the storms strengthened, I am saddened when I think about unbelievers who were watching me offer a poor testimony of the mighty power of God. Can you relate? Perhaps it's not too late. Contact an old friend and let her know what God is doing in your life now, and how faithful He has been to you through the years. Ask God to open the door for a discussion with her about God's plan for her life.

2

David

Stepping Out: Finding Courage to Take Action

LIFE LESSON OF DAVID: In the midst of danger and adversity, David remained focused on the cause of God.

SIGNIFICANCE CONNECTION: Believers must shed fear and personal agendas to focus on and to boldly defend God's cause—the redemption of all of humanity.

Isn't it great fun to take a risk, just for the thrill of the surprise ending? As a senior in high school, I admired a certain young man named Kevin Sowell. He was smart and good-looking, but in my opinion, above me socially, so I watched my dreamboat from afar. As my graduation date neared, I realized I soon would move away and never see any of my classmates again, so I decided to take a risk. I called Mr. Sowell on the phone. "Kevin, this is Kimberly Osborne. Do you know who I am?" He responded that he did. "Well, I'm not doing anything Friday night, and I wondered if you would like to take me out to dinner." Surprisingly, he said yes! He took me to the movies, and then to dinner. When he asked me if I wanted to order dessert, I knew I was in love. When he pulled out a credit card to pay for the bill,

I knew I had to marry him. And three years later, I did! That moment in life was one risk worth taking, and what a wonderful surprise ending!

Most of us don't consider ourselves risk-takers. In fact, we often avoid taking risks at all costs because, after all, when we take a risk we open ourselves up to criticism; we make ourselves vulnerable to the unknown; and we invite the possibility of failure. No one wants to be a failure. Yet one of the greatest failures you and I can experience in our Christian walk happens when we choose to stand still, never willing to take a risk for fear of failure. Standing still or stepping out—that is our choice on our journey to significance.

Standing still is done in silence; stepping out is done with a voice that must be heard for Jesus Christ. Whatever the call, wherever the destination, God will have you standing on the spiritual "X" that marks the spot for an opportunity to share the love and message of Christ.

God is calling you to be a spiritual risk-taker. You have been granted time on this earth to accomplish the will of God, which requires some stepping out. Placing the words *spiritual* and *risk-taker* side by side really creates an oxymoron, because when God calls you to step out in service to Him, He equips you to perform the task; He guides you each step of the way; and He will see the process through to completion. And as you seek to spread the gospel message, the Holy Spirit equips you, guides you, and will be present and working throughout each encounter of your life. No real "risk" is involved when you walk in the center of the Lord's will. But, when God escorts you to the edge of the cliff and gives you the directive to jump, in your flesh it feels very much like a risk, doesn't it?

 Focus on You

What "risk" have you taken lately for God? What were the results? Do you sense God calling you to step out again on faith?

Enter into a time of prayer, asking God to help you learn a life lesson from David and make the significance connection within your own life.

You are the Chosen One

Read 1 Samuel 16:1–13 in your Bible.

Standing still versus stepping out—this was the choice facing the young shepherd boy, David. King Saul reigned as Israel's first God-given earthly king, but Saul soon proved himself to be a weak leader whose heart turned cold toward God. The priest and prophet Samuel mourned over Saul's ungodliness, but God instructed Samuel to rise and go to a little town called Bethlehem. There, Samuel would anoint one of the sons of Jesse to be the next king of Israel. Samuel obeyed the Lord and traveled to Bethlehem, where he sought and found Jesse. As one might imagine, Jesse was more than happy to oblige Samuel's request for a visit, and thus began the parade of Jesse's eight sons before Samuel's eyes.

The first son to come before Samuel was Eliab. As the oldest son, he was the obvious choice to be anointed in the thinking of Samuel, and probably also in the minds of the father Jesse and Eliab himself. Eldest sons held several rights of rank and privilege in Hebrew culture. Samuel beheld Eliab and said, *"Surely the Lord's anointed is before Him!"* (1 Samuel 16:6). But God refused Eliab. God responded with a "hold your horses!" warning to Samuel, revealing a valuable truth of God's acute perception of the heart of every person. The Lord said to Samuel, *"Do not look at his appearance or at his physical stature, because I have refused him. For the Lord does not see as man sees; for man looks at the outward appearance, but the Lord looks at the heart"* (1 Samuel 16:7).

When God looked into the heart of Eliab, He saw a character flaw, some spot on his soul, that rendered Eliab unfit for the position of king. Imagine the bewilderment flying through Eliab's mind, cheeks reddening, as Samuel suddenly withdrew from Eliab and moved on to son number two.

Stepping-Stone

1. Eliab, as the oldest son, was the obvious choice for anointing. Have you ever felt as if you were the obvious choice to be selected for a position, yet didn't get selected? How did you respond to the disappointment?

So it was, when they came, that he looked at Eliab and said, "Surely the Lord's anointed is before Him!"
—1 Samuel 16:6

But the Lord said to Samuel, "Do not look at his appearance or at his physical stature, because I have refused him. For the Lord does not see as man sees; for man looks at the outward appearance, but the Lord looks at the heart."
—1 Samuel 16:7

2. Samuel evaluated Eliab to be "king material" simply from what his eyes could see. How would someone describe you just from looking at your outward appearance? In what points would she be correct? In what points incorrect? From the outward appearance of your life circumstances, would you describe yourself as a likely or an unlikely person for God to choose to spread the gospel?

An Unlikely Selection

So he sent and brought him in. Now he was ruddy, with bright eyes, and good-looking. And the LORD said, "Arise, anoint him; for this is the one!"
—1 Samuel 16:12

Eliab wasn't the only son passed over that day. Samuel examined the seven older sons of Jesse, and God rejected each one as the next king. Samuel knew he had heard God clearly, but he still hadn't anointed a young man's head and was out of sons for selection. Samuel asked Jesse if there wasn't another son from whom he might choose, and Jesse responded that his youngest son was in the field tending the sheep. They sent for the young shepherd, and as David walked through the door, young, ruddy faced, and good-looking, God instructed Samuel, *"Arise, anoint him; for this is the one!"* (1 Samuel 16:12).

Then Samuel took the horn of oil and anointed him in the midst of his brothers; and the Spirit of the LORD came upon David from that day forward.
—1 Samuel 16:13

Talk about being blind sided! You walk in the room from tending the sheep, and standing in the midst of your family is the famous priest, judge, and prophet Samuel, there to anoint one of the Jesse boys to be the next king. And you immediately are seized by Samuel, who is saying God instructs that you, youngest brother, shepherd boy, are the chosen one.

David may have responded like this:

Me? The next king of Israel? Kings have to be authoritative and tell other people what to do. I'm the youngest of eight sons—I never get to tell anyone what to do! I'm sorry; I'm not cut out to be a king.
Or
Sorry, but I am definitely not king material. I'm sure you smelled me when I walked in the room; I hang out with livestock all day! I can't be a king; I don't even have good table manners! Find someone else to do the job.

But David said neither of these things. He humbly accepted the mantle placed upon Him. Samuel anointed David to be the next king, and the Holy Spirit was upon David from that day forward.

Journey TO SIGNIFICANCE

What about you? How do you respond when you feel God tapping you on the shoulder to serve Him in some capacity? Do you humbly accept the call to serve, or do you politely inform God that He picked the wrong person? We tend to determine our ability to do a task based on who else may be available and how their skills measure up to ours. If you look around long enough, you can always find someone who is smarter, better skilled, and more experienced than you to do any task, especially witnessing, and then talk yourself into the idea that the best thing you can do for the kingdom of God is step back and let the "better" person do the work. But when God whispers in your ear that He wants you to serve Him in some way, no one is more perfectly suited than you to complete the task according to God's will. When God calls you to serve, He isn't demanding perfection; otherwise He would have never chosen a human being! What He is looking for is a willing hand and a humble heart.

God's plan of salvation is the most important news, the most powerful message, the most crucial piece of knowledge you will ever attempt to convey to another human being. Does the task seem too daunting? Do you feel the weight of potential failure pulling you into the shadows of insecurity and self-doubt? Consider the recipients of the message; they stand to lose everything of worth, their souls, if you remain silent. God can and will use you if you are willing. If God would choose to use a shepherd boy to be a king, he would choose to use you, no matter what your shortcomings or background, to be an ambassador for Christ. In choosing David, God knew what He was getting for a king. Surely there were other men more stately, more experienced, and better known and respected than David, but God selected a young man of little stature and molded him into king material.

 Stepping-Stone

1. Why are we tempted to compare ourselves to others?

2. Fill in the blanks: *But God has chosen the* _____ *things of the world to put to shame the* _____, *and God has chosen the* _____ *things of the world to put to shame the things which are*

_____; and the _____ things of the world and the things which are despised God has chosen, and the things which are not, to bring to nothing the things that are, that no flesh should _____ in His presence. (1 Corinthians 1:27–29)

3. As a Christian, you are one of God's chosen ones. What has God chosen you to do? List what positions you are certain He has given you, including every role from mother to prayer warrior. Next, pray for discernment concerning any new assignments God may want you to fulfill. Ask the Lord to reveal any God-given roles you may be neglecting or where you are currently "standing still" instead of "stepping out."

What did God see in the heart of David? Perfection? Refinement? Experience? Certainly none of these. But what He did see was a man He could use, a man who would one day be called a man after God's own heart (1 Samuel 13:14). What does God see when He looks in your heart? Surely He sees a few dusty shelves and cobwebbed corners, but if you are a Christian, God looks in your heart and sees the dwelling place of His Spirit. He sees one who has been declared righteous and worthy through the blood of the Savior, Jesus Christ. He sees one of His children, one of His chosen ones.

Looking Beyond What Eyes Can See
In a dusty little forgotten village of Mexico, the people began to gather at the local church. They walked for several blocks in sandaled feet, bundled in worn jackets and faded clothes. They assembled in their cinderblock building, which offered little shelter from the elements because large openings, "windows," welcomed the dust and wind into the church. A young man tuned his guitar and the people rose from their wooden plank benches to sing, "We do not

have much to give, but all we have, we want to give to you, God." They had no resources to speak of, only their love for the Lord and the spiritual gifts God had given them, but with thankful hearts and willing hands, God would indeed work in them and through them to accomplish His will in that dusty village God had not forgotten. Despite the outward appearance of their circumstances, they had embraced their identities as God's chosen ones.

What about you? Have you embraced that identity?

 ## Stepping-Stone

God is the searcher of the heart. He looks beyond what human eyes can see. Read the verses listed below and summarize what each passage reveals about God's knowledge of the human heart. Then, ask God to teach you to see yourself with spiritual eyes, looking beyond the surface, and accepting whatever task God would call you to do.

Jeremiah 17:10

Proverbs 15:11

"I, the LORD, search the heart, I test the mind, even to give every man according to his ways, according to the fruit of his doings."
—Jeremiah 17:10

Hell and Destruction are before the LORD; so how much more the hearts of the sons of men.
—Proverbs 15:11

Eternal Fruitfulness

Jesus said, *"You did not choose Me, but I chose you and appointed you that you should go and bear fruit, and that your fruit should remain"* (John 15:16). When God called you to be His child through a relationship with Jesus Christ, that selection of honor came with an appointment. God has called each of us to live in a manner that we do these two things:

- **Go.** Go where? Wherever He leads. He may lead you across the globe or across the street. He may lead you beside still waters or through a blazing storm. Wherever He leads, you are to go. The Christian life isn't fulfilled on a stationary bike. Marking time isn't on the agenda. Going indicates you are to be in action, never tarrying in a comfortable corner where you feel safe and tucked away from the world.
- **Bear fruit of substance.** Jesus said you are appointed to bear fruit that will remain. The world's given assignments offer rewards that

will rust and wear away, but the rewards of your labors for the Lord bear eternal significance. Imagine the eternal significance of your witness for Jesus Christ. What joy to know that one day you will embrace the loved ones, friends, and neighbors whom you have led to Jesus, standing on the streets of gold together, standing arm in arm as you sing praises to the Holy One!

Like it or not, believe it or not, if you are a Christian, you are God's chosen one. Wherever God leads you, it will be a journey of significance, bearing fruit that will remain.

 Stepping-Stone

What are some of the "fruits that remain" in your life? Read 1 Corinthians 3:11–15 and fill in the categories below.

MY WORKS THAT WILL BURN   MY WORKS THAT WILL ENDURE

David was anointed to be king, Samuel exited to Ramah, and life moved on in Jesse's household. Saul began to have troubles of the mind, and he called upon David to play the harp to soothe his soul. As Saul's harpist, David had to spend most of his days in the house of Saul, except on certain occasions when David was allowed to return home to tend his father's flock. It's here with Jesse that we find David in the next scene of David's life, because Saul and his valiant army had stationed themselves for battle.

Frozen by Fear
Read 1 Samuel 17:1–24 in your Bible.
The Philistine army invaded the land of Judah at the Valley of Elah and

established their camp on a mountain facing one side of the valley. Saul and his men camped on the mountainside opposite them across the valley. On Saul's mountainside, three young men are of particular interest in the army, Jesse's three older sons, including the oldest, Eliab. On the Philistine mountainside, only one man is of named interest, and that's the giant known as Goliath. He was the champion of the Philistine army, and each day he came down out of the mountain and defied the armies of the living God. He dared any man from the Israelite army to enter the valley and fight him man-to-man. Goliath's blasphemies and threats continued day after day, and for 40 consecutive days, a mountainside of men stood still; Israel's army was paralyzed with fear.

And all the men of Israel, when they saw the man, fled from him and were dreadfully afraid.
—1 Samuel 17:24

⟋⟍ Stepping-Stone

1. Consider 1 Samuel 17:24. As a soldier in the army of God, what do you fear most?

2. Men and women who flee feel powerless. Look up the verses below and respond personally to God's words of encouragement. Circle any verses that particularly encourage you in your thoughts about witnessing. You may want to record a verse on a sticky note and place the note somewhere you will see often, such as your bathroom mirror, and resolve to memorize this verse. The next time you have the opportunity to witness, apply God's words of encouragement to help you overcome any anxiety you feel about witnessing.

   Joshua 23:10

   Psalm 18:29

   Isaiah 41:13

   Zechariah 4:6

For God has not given us a spirit of fear, but of power and of love and of a sound mind.
—2 Timothy 1:7

"But you shall receive power when the Holy Spirit has come upon you; and you shall be witnesses to Me in Jerusalem, and in all Judea and Samaria, and to the end of the earth."
—Acts 1:8

And suddenly there came a sound from heaven, as of a rushing mighty wind, and it filled the whole house where they were sitting.
—Acts 2:2

For the weapons of our warfare are not carnal but mighty in God for pulling down strongholds, casting down arguments and every high thing that exalts itself against the knowledge of God, bringing every thought into captivity to the obedience of Christ.
—2 Corinthians 10:4–5

Acts 1:8

Ephesians 3:16

3. Read 2 Timothy 1:7 in the margin. Paul not only tells us what God has *not* given us, a spirit of fear, but just as important, he tells us what God has given us: a spirit of power, of love, and of a sound mind. These three blessings of God overcome fear. Apply these three gifts to your present position on your journey to significance.

Power
Do you sense the power of God in your daily journey? ❏ Yes ❏ No
God's power enables you to speak with authority as you witness to others (Acts 1:8; 2:2).

God's power in your life doesn't grant you authority to control your circumstances. Spend time in prayer, asking God to shield you from fear and worry as you trust Him with all of the circumstances of your life.

Love
Love helps you overcome fear, because love compels you to get beyond yourself and reach out to others. When you think about the next act of "stepping out" God is calling you to do, how will your love for the Lord override your fear of the unknown?

Sound Mind
Your sound mind enables you to identify Satan's lies and schemes in his attempt to bind you with fear. Read 2 Corinthians 10:4–5 in the margin. What negative feelings do you need to eliminate from your thought life to be under the complete authority of Christ? Star those negative feelings that are specifically interfering with your ability to witness for Christ.

An Enemy in the Camp

Read 1 Samuel 17:25–28 in your Bible.

Jesse sent David to the Valley of Elah with provisions for his brothers and their captain, and for David to learn the welfare of his brothers. On the mountainside, David had the occasion to hear the threatening words of the giant, and defiant anger kindled in David's heart. Then David heard the stories of the Israelite men, as they told of King Saul's unsuccessful search for a person to fight the giant; Saul had offered great spoils from the king's treasury for any man willing to take on Goliath. David burst forth with an indignant spirit: *"What shall be done for the man who kills this Philistine and takes away the reproach from Israel? For who is this uncircumcised Philistine, that he should defy the armies of the living God?"* (1 Samuel 17:26).

As David spoke these words of bravery, can you imagine the deafening sound of silence from the men who listened in wonder at the confident words of a young shepherd boy? And who was present to hear the brave remarks of David but big brother Eliab. Eliab's response had some bite of its own: *"Why did you come down here? And with whom have you left those few sheep in the wilderness? I know your pride and the insolence of your heart, for you have come down to see the battle"* (1 Samuel 17:28).

Eliab's words can be divided into three basic messages:

1. *You don't belong here. David, you have come into a camp of warriors, and you are not one! You aren't welcomed here.*
2. *You aren't capable of fighting a giant. Why, we can't even trust you with a few sheep at home! How nice that you want to take on the giant, Little Man, but you are no match for the enemy.*
3. (These were probably the most painful words of all.) *David, your heart isn't right. Your motives aren't pure. You don't want to fight for God; you want glory for yourself.*

As Eliab made his stinging speech to David in front of all the other men, could it be that Eliab was echoing back to David what he had suddenly realized about himself? Could it be, that as Eliab heard the courage in David's spirit, David's words reflected to Eliab a revelation about his own heart? Perhaps Eliab suddenly realized, *I don't belong here; I don't deserve to stand on this mountain as a warrior in God's army.* Second, *I don't feel capable of fighting a giant.* And third, *my heart isn't right with God. My motives for serving in this army aren't pure.*

Stepping-Stone

1. Consider the message in Eliab's words. Do any of his defeating words describe your feelings about witnessing? Consider each statement; then read the Scripture passages that refute the negative thought. In the space provided, apply the Scripture to write a sentence combating each negative thought.

    I don't belong here; I don't deserve to be a warrior in God's army. (See Proverbs 16:9; 1 Corinthians 1:27–29.)

    I don't feel capable. (See Philippians 4:13; 2 Corinthians 12:9.)

    My heart isn't right with God; my motives aren't pure. (See 1 John 1:8–9; Proverbs 16:3.)

2. Are you facing challenges because the enemy, Satan, has shown up at your camp? List specific obstacles you're struggling with; then evaluate whether your responses to these obstacles reflect a working knowledge that the battle is the Lord's.

Eliab had a choice. David's courage shone in stark contrast to what Eliab himself was willing to do. Eliab could have fallen to his knees and asked God to give him the strength and courage to stand beside David as a fellow warrior, but instead, he chose a coward's route and he turned against his own brother. When the call rings forth for the people of God to serve, rest assured, there will be an enemy in the camp.

The men of the Israelite army were a pretense in armor. For 40 days they had gotten up each morning and put on their armor, dressing the part of warriors, realizing they had no intention of doing battle with the giant that day. When the sun went down, perhaps the men sat around camp fires, singing battle hymns and telling glory stories of days gone by, trying to convince one another they were still soldiers, though none were willing to engage in battle with the enemy.

You and I also have a choice. We can show up at church and "dress" the part, but are we willing to engage the enemy in battle for the Lord? Can we stand up and sing with gusto those battle hymns of courage if we know in our hearts we have no intention of ever stepping foot outside the camp to claim territory for God?

Stepping-Stone

Pretense in armor: could it be you? What a deeply personal question to ask yourself; what a chillingly risky choice to allow yourself to examine your words versus your actions, your presentation of yourself at church versus the reality of how you live. Stop. Talk to God. Write down the thoughts He brings to your mind. Be honest with yourself and with God. Find freedom in truth; nothing is hidden from God (1 John 3:20), therefore, none of the inconsistencies of your life are a secret kept from God. The only danger in having this conversation with God is knowing that He will challenge you to live the life of a true warrior for Christ, standing up to giants and proclaiming the truth of the gospel.

If we say that we have no sin, we deceive ourselves, and the truth is not in us. If we confess our sins, He is faithful and just to forgive us our sins and to cleanse us from all unrighteousness.
—1 John 1:8–9

Commit your works to the LORD, and your thoughts will be established.
—Proverbs 16:3

For if our heart condemns us, God is greater than our heart, and knows all things.
—1 John 3:20

Yes, there's an enemy in the camp, *but it's not one another.* Satan is our enemy, but he knows one of his most successful tactics is turning Christians against one another. Goliath was the real enemy in the battle scene at the Valley of Elah, but how interesting that David first had to engage in a war of words with his brother before he could take on the true enemy, the Philistine.

In God's Church today, Christians often fit into one of two categories: the doers and the been-there-and-done-that's, the naysayers of the crowd. Which category best describes you? Are you a David, or are you an Eliab? The needs and characteristics of the lost people of today are different from past generations, creating a giant of a task to reach them with the gospel. Are you open to trying some "out of the box" strategies to share Christ effectively with today's lost person?

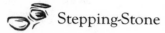 Stepping-Stone

1. As you carefully and prayerfully examine your heart, consider how God might move you to align with His will as a soldier in His army. If you are one who tends to reject others' ideas for new ministry projects or new worship styles, ask God to help you determine your motives. Are you willing to make adjustments in your own life or in the ministry of your church in order to reach the lost in your community? Would you be so bold as to allow God to reveal weaknesses in your heart? Consider some possible reasons for being the naysayer, checking each item that applies to you. Do you:

    ❏ Resent that others might change something you started or that you have cherished through the years?

    ❏ Fear that a group with different ideas will take control and ruin your chances to serve?

    ❏ Fear you will be pressured to participate in a ministry or worship style that makes you feel uncomfortable?

    ❏ Remember a time when your new idea was dismissed, and you're now passing along the painful sting to others?

    ❏ Desire to stay in your comfort zone, no matter what the cost to others?

2. Ephesians 4:29 instructs, *"Let no corrupt word proceed out of your mouth, but what is good for necessary edification, that it may impart grace to the hearers."* Edifying is building up a person to encourage and motivate her to live as Christ. Who has been instrumental in your Christian growth through personal edification? What words encouraged you the most? Contact your encouraging friend to thank her for building you up in the Lord.

3. Hebrews 10:24 says, *"And let us consider one another in order to stir up love and good works."* The word *consider* might involve the notion of planning. Make a plan this week to encourage a sister in Christ whose heart may need some "stirring"! How can you support her in stepping out for the Lord?

As soldiers of God around us answer the call as God's chosen ones, we will inevitably meet fellow Christians with visions and passions very different from our own. We may not feel the call to join them in a ministry endeavor, but woe unto us if we follow Eliab's example and choose to stand in their way as they attempt to obey God's call to go and bear everlasting fruit! At the least, we can support our brothers and sisters in Christ through prayer, and extend genuine friendship and love to them.

Perhaps you are more of a David than an Eliab, and you know the pain of being "put in your place" as you have stepped out and raised your voice. If that's you, take a lesson from David's response to Eliab.

There Is a Cause

Read 1 Samuel 17:29–37 in your Bible.

Oh, the wisdom of God that I wasn't on the mountainside that day! If I had been David, I fear that sarcasm and vindictiveness would have overtaken my tongue. After all, David's brother shamed him in front of an army of macho men! How would David save his dignity? I might have been tempted to tell Eliab, tongue in cheek, how right he was, that he really was the better man for the job, and I and all of these men standing around would support him wholeheartedly as we watched him march into the valley to fight Goliath. *Go on, now, Eliab, you're the man; you know we've got your back!* But David responded in wisdom, making the difficult choice to show great spiritual maturity. He chose not to let Eliab's demeaning words draw him into a personal confrontation. David knew the issue wasn't about him! He knew the focus wasn't on whose armor was shiniest or whose shield was heaviest, but the battle belonged to the Lord.

David responded to Eliab, *"What have I done now? Is there not a cause?"* (1 Samuel 17:29). What a poignant question for David to ask. What a timeless question that we should all be asking ourselves: *Is there not a cause?*

What is the cause of God? We find it throughout Scripture, from Genesis to Revelation, but can we articulate God's cause? Perhaps a familiar verse, John 3:16, best summarizes God's cause:

And David said, "What have I done now? Is there not a cause?"
—1 Samuel 17:29

For God so loved the world that He gave His only begotten Son, that whoever believes in Him should not perish but have everlasting life.
—John 3:16

- **For God:** The cause is all about God. It begins with God and it ends with God. God is the author of the cause, He is the initiator of the cause, and without God, there is no cause.

- **So loved:** God's cause is motivated by love. Have you given pause to absorb this beautiful truth? God's cause is not to create robots or fearful servants. He isn't a manipulative God like many false religions paint Him to be. God loves us, frail and fickle creatures that we are. Paul reminds us of the depths of God's love as he points us to the vivid picture of God's love in action: *"but God demonstrates His own love toward us, in that while we were still sinners, Christ died for us"* (Romans 5:8).

- **The world:** The cause is for you and for me. The cause extends to your neighbors, family, and friends. God's cause is for the people on the other side of the globe who despise you because of the flag you live under, and it's for the person who sells drugs to the children who attend your local school. God's cause is for everyone. How can we get on board with God's cause, seeking to reach even these who are so unlovable to us? We must pray for God's love and compassion to flow through us, and we must ask ourselves, *where would I be if it were not for the grace of God in my life?*

- **That He gave His only begotten Son:** God's mission can and will succeed, because God gave His Son. God believes in the cause so much that He gave the most precious gift He could give, Jesus, to be our supreme sacrifice. What are you willing to give for God's cause?

- **That whoever:** Give praise to a God who would include even you. *"Blessed be the God and Father of our Lord Jesus Christ, who has blessed us with every spiritual blessing in the heavenly places in Christ, just as He chose us in Him before the foundation of the world, that we should be holy and without blame before Him in love"* (Ephesians 1:3–4).

- **Believes in Him:** At the center of the cause is Jesus, so Jesus must be our focus. On your life's journey, don't be deceived by the world's definition of significance. Your significance lies not in getting people to admire you or agree with you, nor are you here to get people behind your agenda or your cause. Your significance is found in getting people focused on Christ, agreeing with God's truths, adoring the Father, and getting people beside you, shoulder to shoulder, at the foot of the cross.

- **Should not perish:** We love to think about the vast beauty of heaven. My six-year-old daughter loves to sing Southern gospel songs with me in the car, and many of our favorite tunes tell of heaven's glory. Julia asks me why there's no night in heaven, and what we'll be doing there, and I don't have all of the answers. I can't even understand myself how heaven can last forever and forever and forever, but I believe it will. Along with that promise from Scripture, we also must face God's revelation that hell is a real place of unspeakable horror that will last forever and forever and forever. People who die without having Jesus as their Savior will exist in this never-ending torment. How does that move you? Every moment of your day, someone somewhere is dying, slipping into an eternal hell. That's why we can't afford the time to bicker and squabble about whose ideas are greatest and what tempo of music we will worship to, or to retreat into the shadows of fearfulness or complacency as we refuse to answer the call of God, because the cause is too desperate for those who are perishing.

- **But have everlasting life:** God's cause? To lovingly hold every man, woman, boy, and girl in fellowship with Him by His grace as we walk through this world, and to usher us into His eternal kingdom where the fellowship never ends.

Every one of us has a cause. You may not have a formal cause that you've written in your journal, but your daily agenda and personal motivations reveal your cause in life. God will not move to get in line with your cause; you have to find Him and get aligned with His will. Your journey to significance will entail living out a particular role assigned to you by God, which is your contribution to fulfilling God's cause. Your role may require great personal sacrifice, but no other lifestyle could satisfy your soul more than abiding in His perfect will for your life.

 Stepping-Stone

Read 1 Samuel 17:31–37, the account of David's conversation with King Saul.

1. Saul first reacted negatively to David's offer to fight. Saul told David he wasn't capable of fighting the enemy, a message David had already heard once from Eliab. Are you easily discouraged when others question your abilities?

Now when the words which David spoke were heard, they reported them to Saul; and he sent for him. Then David said to Saul, "Let no man's heart fail because of him; your servant will go and fight with this Philistine." And Saul said to David, "You are not able to go against this Philistine to fight with him; for you are a youth, and he a man of war from his youth." But David said to Saul, "Your servant used to keep his father's sheep, and when a lion or a bear came and took a lamb out of the flock, I went out after it and struck it, and delivered the lamb from its mouth; and when it arose against me, I caught it by its beard, and struck and killed it. Your servant has killed both lion and bear; and this uncircumcised Philistine will be like one of them, seeing he has defied the armies of the living God." Moreover David said, "The LORD, who delivered me from the paw of the lion and from the paw of the bear, He will deliver me from the hand of this Philistine." And Saul said to David, "Go, and the LORD be with you!"
—1 Samuel 17:31–37

2. In verse 37, David didn't respond to Saul with accolades of his brute strength, but with a testimony of God's past faithfulness to give him victory over his enemy. What has been God's track record in your life?

Standing Still or Stepping Out

Read 1 Samuel 17:40–54 in your Bible.

Saul granted David permission to fight the giant. David descended from the mountainside into the valley, and the Israelite men who stood behind him surely stood in perfect silence. Goliath despised the puny stature of this so-called opponent, calling David's weaponry a stick fit only for a dog's game of fetch. Can you hear the roar of laughter and see the confident posture of the eager Philistines, watching with hands anxious for bloodshed? David once again proved by his words that he knew the cause wasn't about Him, but almighty God. He responded boldly to Goliath: *"You come to me with a sword, with a spear, and with a javelin. But I come to you in the name of the LORD of hosts, the God of the armies of Israel, whom you have defied. This day the LORD will deliver you into my hand, and I will strike you and take your head from you. And this day I will give the carcasses of the camp of the Philistines to the birds of the air and the wild beasts of the earth, that all the earth may know that there is a God in Israel"* (1 Samuel 17:45–46).

 Stepping-Stone

1. David declared that he came to do battle in the name of the Lord (v. 45). Identify the attributes of the name of the Lord revealed in the following verses:

   Proverbs 18:10

   Malachi 1:11

   Acts 3:16

2. Read 1 Samuel 17:46–47. David knew that personal victories are for the glory of God. Write a prayer below, expressing your desire that God's

glory be revealed as He brings victory in your personal trials. Ask God to help you demonstrate His powerful existence through your personal lifestyle of sharing Christ with others.

With a shepherd's sling, David killed the giant with a stone to the forehead. As the giant fell, the Philistines probably stood for a moment in disbelief, but then the enemy did what the enemy always does when it sees the hand of God—they turned and ran. And for the first time in 40 days, a sea of men, the Israelite army, found their voices again. They ran down the mountain into the valley to chase their enemies to their deaths, crying out with eager warriors' cries, having seen with their eyes God was indeed on their side.

But if we may take a bit of poetic license, perhaps there was yet one man standing still on the mountainside that day—big brother Eliab. Did he stand still, mouth agape, staring down into the valley as he watched his youngest brother remove the head of a giant, and ask himself, *What did David just do?* Then, *What did God just do?* And then, a realization that would haunt him the rest of his life: *It could have been me.*

"For the eyes of the Lord run to and fro throughout the whole earth, to show Himself strong on behalf of those whose heart is loyal to Him" (2 Chronicles 16:9). As God casts His eyes upon you, will He find you stepping out or standing still? It's a significant choice.

 Retracing Your Steps to Stay on Course

LIFE LESSON OF DAVID: In the midst of danger and adversity, David remained focused on the cause of God.

When I find myself in the midst of adversity, I usually focus on _____

_____

_____

Write God's cause in your own words. Plan to talk with at least one Christian friend today about what God's cause is based on what God has said in the Bible.

SIGNIFICANCE CONNECTION: Believers must shed fear and personal agendas to focus on and boldly defend God's cause—the redemption of all of mankind.

To support God's cause to bring all people to salvation, I want to release to God my fear of _____
and my selfish opinions about _____
_____ .

Identify ways you are working toward God's cause of bringing all people to know Jesus as Savior and Lord.

1.

2.

3.

4.

Identify new ways you would like to work toward God's cause of bringing all people to know Jesus as Savior and Lord.

1.

2.

3.

4.

Stepping Up to the Challenge

God has granted great favor to you as a believer. Make a list of the many privileged titles you bear as a Christian, including redeemed, forgiven, cherished, gifted, chosen, commissioned, and so forth. Spend time in prayer, communicating with God about each of these titles and what they mean in your life. Ask God to help you operate in the power and favor He has granted to you, courageously stepping out for Him on your journey to significance.

3

Mary
of Bethany

Taking Time to Refuel: Intimacy with the Savior

LIFE LESSON OF MARY: Mary's greatest longing was to be in Jesus's presence.

SIGNIFICANCE CONNECTION: Our witness for Christ begins and is sustained through a growing, vibrant relationship with Jesus Christ.

I have three very young children. Naturally, mine is a life of leisure. Not! Unfortunately for my children and saintly husband, I could give the Energizer Bunny a run for his money. Sure, he steadily plods along looking cool in his shades, but me, no way, I am doing anything and everything at a fast pace, a *frenzied* pace most days, and looking far cooler than that Energizer Bunny because I'm donning shades *and* high heels! Oh, it's great vacuuming up crumbs and stirring vegetable soup at the same time, then coaching my five-year-old to snap her fingers while transferring clothes from the washer to the dryer with a baby on one hip, but what is the end result of all this hyperactivity from Mom? What happens to my patience when someone spills juice on his shirt, an unscheduled event that throws us three minutes late for church, or when a tiny voice asks for cuddle time at the precise moment I'm scheduled to unload the dishwasher? What happens when I jump through hoops for 30 minutes of "alone" time, and I hear the voice of God wooing me for quality time with Him in His Word, yet stacks of paperwork are calling out to me from the bottom of my desk?

When you want to honor God but you operate throughout the day as though your true goal in life is to squeeze in as many chores and activities as possible without landing in a rubber room, who wins?

I was driving my three little tots to "wee" school one morning, and my daughter Julia and I were talking about the song playing on the Christian radio station. "Mommy, what's that song about?" She was listening intently to a song describing the great sacrifice Jesus made on the cross. I answered her question and then listened to her explain to me in great detail all that she knew about the crucifixion of our Savior. By the time I had pulled the car into a parking space at wee school, the clock was telling on me for being four minutes late. Bummer. Julia had just begun a fresh discourse on how Mary must have felt as she watched Jesus dying on the cross, when into my mind popped my next sentence I would interject into the conversation when Julia would eventually pause momentarily to breathe: *Julia, I really want to talk with you about this, but right now we need to get you to your classroom.*

Hold up! Stop! Was I about to tell my precious firstborn child that we're in too big of a hurry to talk about the Savior of the world paying for our sins on a cruel cross? And we're in a hurry because they need to get inside and play, and I need to get home and check my email? I caught that sentence just before it spilled out of my mouth to leave a nasty stain on my daughter's heart. I had to go home and spend some time meditating on my priorities and how they were affecting the people around me.

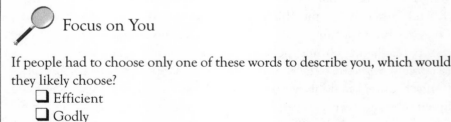 Focus on You

If people had to choose only one of these words to describe you, which would they likely choose?
- ❏ Efficient
- ❏ Godly
- ❏ Dependable
- ❏ Busy

Which word do you desire as the chosen descriptor of you, and why?

Enter into a time of prayer, asking God to help you learn a life lesson from Martha and to make the significance connection within your own life.

Queen of the Church Social
Read Luke 10:38–42 in your Bible.

Mary is our center of focus for this chapter, but for clarity as well as a smidge of entertainment, let's first develop Martha, to draw a contrast between her and Mary, her beloved sister. Martha of Bethany is an intriguing character, and we might say she's the forerunner of our now modern-day Martha in the kitchen, Martha Stewart. Many women are self-described Martha-types; some take on the role by design, and others just to keep up with the demands of womanhood.

If you know any Martha-types, surely you'll agree that they are nothing if not consistent. For instance, you know it's a Martha entering the grocery store, because she's armed with her coupons in one hand and her checkbook in the other, and she already has the coupons arranged aisle by aisle in which she will find the grocery items as she walks through the store. And a Martha will *always* count her groceries *before* getting into the 20-items-or-less lane! Now, don't you like that about a Martha? Incidentally, she will also count the grocery items in *your* buggy before *you* enter the 20-items-or-less lane!

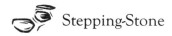 Stepping-Stone

Take a short quiz just for fun to determine how Martha-ish you really are!

1. For my quiet time, I:
   a. Usually do the same routine each day.
   b. Enjoy a variety of methods of worship.
   c. Oops! I've been too busy lately to have quiet time with God.

2. My approach to serving God is:
   a. I feel so comfortable doing the same things that I sometimes forget to pray about my ministry; I just jump in and start doing it.

    b.   I rely on God each step of the way because I need His strength and wisdom.

    c.   Piece of cake! I can do this stuff with my eyes closed!

3.   When I sit through a Bible lesson:

    a.   I sometimes only half listen, because most of what is being said I've heard before.

    b.   I ask God to let me hear His voice, and I try to gather new insights from the Scripture.

    c.   Been there, done that. I let my eyes glaze over and make a mental shopping list for next year's Vacation Bible School materials.

(a = 1 point; b = 0 points; c = 2 points)

Points:

Under 2:   You are a "Mary"! (Either that, or you are a Martha in denial.)

2-3:   Buy a T-shirt with the following words emblazoned across your chest: *Martha-in-training.*

4-6:   Yep, you're a Martha-type. I'm surprised you spared the time to take this silly quiz when you could have been polishing your bathroom faucet!

Martha-types generally are consistent, but maybe you tend to be more Martha in some settings more than others. On a scale from 1 to 10, how Martha are you:

At home?   1 2 3 4 5 6 7 8 9 10

At work?   1 2 3 4 5 6 7 8 9 10

At church/ministry?   1 2 3 4 5 6 7 8 9 10

Martha of Bethany was a go-getter, a doer, a mover, and a shaker, and for these admirable personality traits, many women can relate to her. If Martha could be zapped into the present, wouldn't she be the best vacation Bible school director ever to design craft-stick displays of Noah's Ark? Or even the best church social director ever to spread a tablecloth in the fellowship hall? Martha would have the desserts color-coordinated and alphabetized, but they would be beautifully represented on the table nonetheless, because that's the way some Marthas operates. Many thanks belong to the Marthas of the world. They are the women who notice a need and don't wait for a personal invitation to get involved; instead, they roll up their sleeves and get the job done well and on time, because Marthas are determined, driven women who thrive on completing checklists. Marthas will remain faithful to a task until it's completed, no matter how laborious, how tedious, how mundane the project becomes, *and* no matter how miserable they make themselves and sometimes others. As a result of their unfailing desire to make the world a better place, (well, at least a more organized place,) Marthas often shoulder the burden of responsibility in the workplace, and even in the home and the church. So, what's the matter with Martha? What's so special about Mary?

If we're honest with ourselves, perhaps we have difficulty relating to Mary. Maybe there's a part of us, deep down in the recesses of our souls that wants to take up for Martha, even if it's just a little bit. After all, the Son of God showed up at her door, and peanut butter sandwiches simply wouldn't do! Any of us would surely want to whip up a soufflé and fold cloth napkins into the shape of swans for the King of kings and Lord of lords. And if Mary had joined her in the kitchen, they quickly could have completed the work, and stayed up all night long talking with Jesus *after* the meal, *after* the chores were done. That scenario seems right to us, doesn't it? It seems fair, and we want God to be fair. God *is* fair, but not as we define fairness. God's distinct superiority in thoughts over mankind's is recorded in 1 Samuel 16:7. *"For the LORD does not see as man sees; for man looks at the outward appearance, but the LORD looks at the heart."* There's more to this story than meets the eye. Jesus could see beyond the busy hands of Martha to surmise the full scope of what was transpiring in her heart.

 Stepping-Stone

1. After reading the scenario in Luke 10:38–42, write below what you think was Martha's heart issue.

2. Jesus wasn't praising Mary for lounging, nor rebuking Martha because of the work she had done, for faith without works is dead (James 2:17). In fact, many of the female followers of Jesus ministered to Him on a regular basis (Matthew 27:55; Luke 8:1–3). God desires a strong work ethic from each of His children. What is the message in the following verses?

Proverbs 10:4

Proverbs 13:4

Proverbs 22:29

Ecclesiastes 9:10

On Your Feet or On Your Knees

The Lord praised Mary for where she chose to position herself, for she had chosen "that good part." Positionally, exactly where was Mary? Mary was at the feet of Jesus, a sign of humility and submission in her culture, acknowledging Jesus's lordship in her life.

What was Mary doing while she sat at Jesus's feet? She was listening to His words. We don't know what Jesus was discussing with the disciples in this passage. Perhaps He was giving a discourse on Moses, sharing favorite experiences from that day's ministry, giving instructions for tomorrow, or speaking a parable. Nor did Mary know what Jesus would be discussing when she first positioned herself at His feet, but she knew Jesus was the kind of man, the kind of *God*, who did not waste words. We can be certain that all Jesus said was worthy of interest, and Mary had given Jesus her full attention.

Though a lowly woman in a male-dominated culture, Mary felt welcomed at the feet of Jesus. What an honor, what a special status, that God's Son would allow Mary such a closeness to Him to draw near boldly without a moment of fear or hesitation. Likewise, we also may come boldly into God's presence. *"Therefore, brethren, having boldness to enter the Holiest by the blood of Jesus, . . . let us draw near with a true heart in full assurance of faith"* (Hebrews 10:19, 22a). Jesus would bid you to come. Jesus would have you feel drawn to the safety of His holy presence. In nearness to God, you'll find a consistent, calming wash of comfort, yet you'll also find God using that time you spend with Him to propel you into greater service for the kingdom of God. Nearness to God is a blessing. It's a quiet comfort. It's a strengthening and a renewing process. It's taking time to refuel.

In contrast, Luke wrote that Martha was distracted, more literally, *drawn away*. In order for Martha to be drawn away, she was intended to be in one location, but somehow ended up somewhere else. Martha made a conscious decision when she invited Jesus into her home and shut the door behind Him. She decided she would feel more comfortable on her feet in the kitchen than on her knees in the living room, listening to the words of Jesus. Martha was *drawn away* from the feet of Jesus, *drawn away* from positioning herself in complete submission to Him, and she was *drawn away* from the very words of the Son of God. Routine busyness was the great enticement she allowed to draw her away from the Lord.

Stepping-Stone

1. What may be currently distracting or drawing you away from Jesus? What are you doing about it?

2. Are you currently experiencing a sweet intimacy with Jesus Christ, or are you spiritually dry? Reflect on those times in your life when you've felt closest to Jesus. How would you describe your life during those times of greatest intimacy with the Savior?

    What habits were you exercising in your quiet time spent with Him?

> *Therefore, brethren, having boldness to enter the Holiest by the blood of Jesus, . . . let us draw near with a true heart in full assurance of faith.*
> —Hebrews 10:19, 22a

- Did you approach your quiet time with God as if it were another item on the "to-do" list to complete swiftly, or did you consider that time as a necessary privilege to prepare for the day's living?

- Were you more or less likely to talk about God and His goodness during the day?

- Were you more or less eager to tell others about Christ?

The Dangers of the Routine

The kitchen was Martha's safe-haven, requiring no real thought or extra effort from her. Perhaps Martha thought, *Welcome the men, feed the men, clean up after the men—got it! That's my part for the kingdom of God!* Her ministry had become little more than a routine. Routine feels comfortable to us, but marching to that familiar beat can lead us down a path of service with an unplugged heart. When we are attempting to serve God out of obligation, clinging to familiarity, and in our own strength, we can expect resentment, burnout, and misery to result from our empty efforts.

You probably know many Christians who are in a spiritual rut, and they don't like it, but they have no idea how to get out. Perhaps they don't realize there's a more fulfilling life available; perhaps they don't get what other Christians are so excited about and pass it off as phony, slobbery sentimentalism. Those who shake their heads and mutter their negative criticism, "I just don't get it," travel their walk with Christ in a rut. What an outrageous waste, when sweet, close fellowship with Christ is available to all who would draw near to sit at His feet.

For indeed, those who are far from You shall perish; You have destroyed all those who desert You for harlotry. But it is good for me to draw near to God; I have put my trust in the Lord GOD, that I may declare all Your works.
—Psalm 73:27–28

 Stepping-Stone

1. Read Psalm 73:28. How do you draw near to God? How does trusting God as your refuge relate to letting go of your routine methods of service?

2. Now read Psalm 73:27. Describe how clinging to the routine is a form of spiritual unfaithfulness.

3. Is it possible to allow your witness for Christ to become routine? Why or why not?

Martha strikes us as a woman who could have prepared a meal for a crowd of hungry men with her eyes closed. Serving Jesus and His friends was a routine action for Martha, something she could do with little thought or emotion. What about your current areas of service? Have your ministry actions become so routine that you could perform them with your eyes closed? As a result of the familiarity, are you performing them with your *heart* closed?

Routine can also lead us down a path of serving with our ears closed. Martha didn't feel any need to hear what Jesus was talking about to the others. Did she believe she had heard it all before? That there was nothing new He could say to her? That she already had landed where she needed to be spiritually, so she was justified to plug into her familiar spot and put her mind on "cruise"?

God is not about stagnant, routine lifestyles. *"Behold, I will do a new thing, now it shall spring forth; shall you not know it?"* (Isaiah 43:19). Sadly, no, we won't know about the new thing God is offering us if we aren't looking for God to move us beyond our routine service. When our eyes are focused on the assembly-line operations of life—washing laundry, preparing dinner, filling out reports, paying bills, praying scantily over a pre-prepared prayer list, halfheartedly reading two verses of Scripture a day, doing just enough to get by as a Sunday School teacher—we needn't be surprised that we can't seem to muster up the energy or want-to to reach out into our world to make a difference for Christ. It will be no surprise that we can't seem to find any lost people to share Christ with, or any hurting people who need us to be the hands and feet of Christ. And ironically, we can get so robotic in our

"Behold, I will do a new thing, now it shall spring forth; shall you not know it?"
—Isaiah 43:19a

But his delight is in the law of the LORD, and in His law he meditates day and night. He shall be like a tree planted by the rivers of water, that brings forth its fruit in its season, whose leaf also shall not wither; and whatever he does shall prosper.
—Psalm 1:2–3

spiritual routines, we may not even notice how ineffective we've become for the kingdom of God. Precious sister, hear God crying out with thundering echoes through the canyons of your soul, *Let me be a vital part of your life! Let me bless you, teach you, nourish your soul, strengthen your spirit, define your agenda, sharpen your focus, initiate your resolve!*

Stepping-Stone

Read Psalm 1:2–3 and interact with these verses to understand more fully the blessed woman's ways.

But his delight is in the law of the LORD.

Delight suggests to me the word picture of bending toward. We can expect joy when we choose to bend our will toward the instruction of God. If bending is necessary, that means the will must have a natural desire toward something else: the flesh.

1. What fleshly desires are most likely to stand in the way of you spending time refueling from God?

2. What results do you expect from quiet retreat with God?
   ❑ A sense of relief by fulfilling an obligation
   ❑ Chastisement and shame
   ❑ A challenge from God to reach further into the world to reach the lost
   ❑ Other: _____

In His law he meditates day and night.

Because of the influence of far eastern religions, we sometimes confuse biblical references to meditation with the practice of going into an odd trancelike state. Instead, meditation in this verse means to mutter or to make sounds with your mouth, sort of like talking to yourself. Perhaps you already talk to yourself on a regular basis! But verse 2 specifically describes talking to yourself about God's law. Your mind is constantly forming thoughts. When you mull over God's Word in your mind under the Holy Spirit's direction, using God's Word as a filter for your actions and reactions to the events of your day, you gain a greater understanding, remembrance, and application of God's Word.

3. Look up Jeremiah 15:16 and write it below. Read the verse carefully, examining how accurately you could say those words to the Lord. Ask God to renew your passion for His Word.

He shall be like a tree planted by the rivers of water, that brings forth its fruit in its season, whose leaf also shall not wither; and whatever he does shall prosper (Psalm 1:3).

When your life is consistently irrigated by the living water God pours into your soul through drawing near to Him for fellowship and Scripture meditation, you will be a vibrant, productive Christian. Doesn't every Martha have a burning desire to be productive? But you can't be productive for the kingdom of God, bearing spiritual fruit, if you aren't firmly fed from the roots by the living God. Notice the fruit is specific to that tree ("its") and the fruit comes in season; Marthas don't want seasons of fruit, they want to dig down deeper to be the only apple tree on the block bearing fruit twelve months a year! Paul says, *"When I am weak, then I am strong"* (2 Corinthians 12:10); when you realize you can do nothing of worth in your own strength and choose to submit to God, then you will bear the sweetest version of fruit with the power to turn your corner of the world upside down for Jesus Christ.

Have you ever watched a Christian wither on the vine? She was on fire for the Lord, involved in several ministries, running swiftly in the name of the Lord, but then suddenly she dropped out of church without any explanation. Doing the Lord's work is a great privilege, but also such a challenge. Delight in God's law and meditate on it around the clock, and you will have healthy leaves kept fresh and green from the sustaining power of Jesus. You will prosper, not wither, on the True Vine.

4. If you could select one arena you would like to prosper in, maybe your first choice would be writing or making money or power shopping, but let's be kingdom minded for a moment and choose prospering as a witness for Jesus Christ. Would you like to be prosperous in sharing your

faith? What would that look like in the life of a believer? Looking at the details of Psalm 1:2–3, what would be a necessary habit for someone who is effectively sharing her faith with others?

Kitchen Help Recruits

Reread Luke 10:38–42 in your Bible.

As Martha entered the kitchen to stir up those food items in her pots and pans, we can imagine she was also stirring up a bit of righteous indignation in her heart. *Oh, that lazy sister of mine. What an embarrassment she is to the family! I have tried and tried to work on my sister. If only she would work as hard as I do, maybe we could get some things done around here!*

Have you ever had such a thought? In a modern context, perhaps the thought would be more like this: *If only the other women in my circle group would show up and be committed like me,* **maybe** *we could get some things done around here! Or If only the other families in this church would tithe as faithfully as my family,* **maybe** *we could get some things done around here!* Does this poem summarize our secret inward beliefs:

> What a better place the world would be
> If the entire world could be like me!

Can you imagine in your mind's eye how Martha might have peered around the corner of the kitchen into the living area to get her sister's attention? *"Mary! Mary! I know you hear me! Get in here!"* When Martha had reached her boiling point in the kitchen, she then marched into the living area (we might suppose) and proceeded to interrupt Jesus! She apparently was quite sure that what she was about to accomplish in her sister's life to teach her a lesson in serving was more significant than anything Jesus might have been accomplishing in Mary's life at that moment.

Next Martha asked a compelling question: *"Lord, do you not care?"* (Luke 10:40). Notice her choice of wording, spoken in such a negative tone. Martha's heart was filled with frustration and bitterness because she felt overworked and underappreciated, a sure sign when serving the Lord that you're serving in your own strength or from a wrong motivation, following your own agenda.

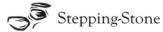 Stepping-Stone

1. Have you ever felt like you weren't getting enough help and support at home? At work? At church? How did you respond?

2. Martha felt justified in her anger with Mary. Consider these three examples of when religious leaders found fault with Jesus, listed below. What was the issue in each example? Do you suppose the leaders sincerely believed they were justified in their "righteous indignation"?

   Matthew 9:11

   Matthew 12:1–2

   Mark 2:6–7

3. Choosing the good part includes not allowing others to pressure you into getting busy in order to meet their expectations of what a Christian lifestyle should look like. How will you overcome the temptation to yield to the Martha-esque "kitchen help recruits" in your life? Write a prayer below, expressing to God your desire to please Him more than any person in your life.

That Good Part

Martha assumed she had made the right decision about where Jesus wanted her. Why else would she have barged into the area where the Lord was talking,

And when the Pharisees saw it, they said to His disciples, "Why does your Teacher eat with tax collectors and sinners?"
—Matthew 9:11

At that time Jesus went through the grainfields on the Sabbath. And His disciples were hungry, and began to pluck heads of grain and to eat. And when the Pharisees saw it, they said to Him, "Look, Your disciples are doing what is not lawful to do on the Sabbath!"
—Matthew 12:1–2

And some of the scribes were sitting there and reasoning in their hearts, "Why does this Man speak blasphemies like this? Who can forgive sins but God alone?"
—Mark 2:6–7

interrupt Him, and then tell Him what to do? *"Tell her to help me."* she demanded (Luke 10:40). Perhaps Martha was frustrated with Jesus for not speaking up before she had to initiate it; or maybe she assumed Jesus had noticed what Martha would have called Mary's thoughtlessness, but Jesus was too polite of a houseguest to embarrass Mary. However, instead of agreeing with Martha, Jesus offered Martha a gentle rebuke. We can almost hear the slight indignant gasp out of Martha's mouth, followed by a very long, very awkward pause.

Jesus had no reason to question Mary's loving devotion. Would a woman who chose to sit at His feet, clinging to His every word, be the sort of woman who would allow Jesus to go hungry? Surely not. Nor was Jesus questioning Martha's loyalty. Jesus likely showed up unannounced with several other men, and regardless of the time of day, we know men are always hungry, yet Martha never hesitated to welcome them in with a smile. Not only was her hospitality inconvenient, but it also was dangerous; Jesus was already a wanted man in Jerusalem, just two miles away from her home in Bethany. Martha was a committed follower of Christ, but Jesus wanted more from her than hospitality. Martha's angry reaction to Mary, along with her pointed words directed toward Jesus, revealed her lack of heart connection to the Master. Her walk with God had become about doing service, but not about serving out of a heart of love. Martha must have been truly floored when Jesus called Mary's choice "that good part." What could be better than Martha's method of serving? The "better part" required sitting still, not stirring; meditating, not meddling; listening, not lashing out; personal spiritual growth, not personal agenda growth. "That good part" had everything to do with the greatest motive of God in creating mankind—the good part was about nurturing that spiritual component of self that grows and flourishes when connected in an intimate relationship with the Creator. What Jesus wanted Martha to know, and what He wants you and me to know, dear friend, is that God's first calling on your life is relationship.

Throughout history, or "past tense," God has desired so greatly to have fellowship with us that He has reached down through the expanse of space and time to reveal Himself to us, extending the privilege that we might know Him and enter into a relationship with Him. In the beginning, God walked with Adam and Eve in the cool of the evening (Genesis 3:8), having fellowship with them. Noah was privileged to walk with God (Genesis 6:9). Enoch walked with God (Genesis 5:22, 24). Abraham was called the friend of God (James 2:23). God spoke to Moses *"as a man speaks to his friend"* (Exodus 33:11). We see the picture of relationship with God, nurtured by fellowship, even in the words of Jesus: *"Behold, I stand at the door and knock. If anyone hears My voice and opens the door, I will come in to him and dine with him, and he with Me"* (Revelation 3:20).

Now consider future tense. We like to think about heaven with its streets of gold as a place of eternal reward for us, and heaven indeed will be one incredible gift from our Father who loves us and knows how to give good gifts. But don't miss the bigger picture of what God has established: God is going to transform us with a new body, free of sin, so that He can have an unhindered relationship with us and spend eternal "time" with us. Wow! What love!

 Stepping-Stone

Fill in the blanks for these verses of Scripture to see how God has chosen to bless us with intimate fellowship with Him in the present.

Do you not know that you are the _____ of God and that the Spirit of God _____ in you?
—1 Corinthians 3:16

By this we know that we _____ in Him, and He in us, because He has given us of His _____.
—1 John 4:13

Worried and Troubled

Jesus told Martha she was worried and troubled over many things, none of which fell into the category of "that good part." What has you worried and troubled? Is it "stuff," such as piles of paperwork or clothes in the dryer? Is it people, trying to figure out how to force people to live up to your expectations? Be kind to your troubled mind. Choose "that good part" today, and open your heart to serve God from the outflow of sweet fellowship with Him. When ministry is fueled by love for Jesus, there's nothing routine, and nothing bitter, about it.

Imagine this scene on the stage at Bethany. Jesus sits at center stage, Mary positioned lovingly at His feet, while disciples flank Jesus on either side. Martha stands boldly, hands on her hips, dangerously close to stealing center stage from Jesus. Martha states her case while Mary lowers her head, then she slowly looks into the eyes of Jesus to hear what her Master expects of her. Jesus replies to Martha's complaint with a soft rebuke, and then...the curtain slowly descends on that scene, and we never learn here how Martha responds.

But what's more important is how you will respond. The scene has unfolded before your eyes, and surely you see your own character somewhere on that stage. How will you respond to the words of Jesus? Will you pursue "that good part"?

 ## Stepping-Stone

1. Read Proverbs 15:32 in the margin. How will you respond to what God is teaching you in this chapter? What will you do when you feel tempted to put your spiritual life on autopilot, content to stay in a routine of the familiar rather than moving forward spiritually?

2. Read Ecclesiastes 4:6 in the margin. How does this verse relate to having a Mary lifestyle? How could having "both hands full" interfere your effectiveness to be a vibrant, active witness for Jesus Christ?

3. If God is convicting your heart to spend some quiet time talking with Him, mark your place and set your workbook aside. In whatever remaining time you were going to devote to this chapter today, yield that time to sit quietly with Jesus. Listen for Him to speak to your heart.

Casting All Your Cares Upon Him
Read John 11:1–4 in your Bible.

Lazarus, Mary, and Martha had special relationships with Jesus. They had witnessed the power of the Lord, they had grown from the wisdom of the Lord, and they had experienced the love of the Lord Jesus. John 11:5 records, *"Now*

He who disdains instruction despises his own soul, but he who heeds rebuke gets understanding.
—Proverbs 15:32

Better a handful with quietness than both hands full, together with toil and grasping for the wind.
—Ecclesiastes 4:6

Now a certain man was sick, Lazarus of Bethany, the town of Mary and her sister Martha. It was that Mary who anointed the Lord with fragrant oil and wiped His feet with her hair, whose brother Lazarus was sick. Therefore the sisters sent to Him, saying, "Lord, behold, he whom You love is sick." When Jesus heard that, He said, "This sickness is not unto death, but for the glory of God, that the Son of God may be glorified through it."
—John 11:1–4

Jesus loved Martha and her sister and Lazarus." Thinking about the marvelous ways of Jesus the Savior, it's easy to love our Lord. But praise God, how amazing is the grace of God that He also loves us with an unfailing love!

When Lazarus became seriously ill, Mary and Martha sent a simple message: *"He whom You love is sick"* (John 11:3). Mary and Martha didn't make any demands of Jesus. Traveling to Bethany, so close to Jerusalem, would place Jesus in danger. Mary and Martha knew that Jesus could make the sick well again without being physically present, for He had performed such a long-distance miracle in the nobleman's son at Capernaum (John 4:46–54). Mary and Martha displayed great faith by expressing Lazarus's need to Jesus and trusting Him to resolve the situation. (Let's give Martha credit for not attempting to tell Jesus what to do this time!)

When you face a problem that is clearly bigger than you, what better choice could you make than to turn it over to Jesus and say, "Lord, I don't have a clue what to do with this ugly mess. It's yours, Lord. I trust *You* to deal with it!"

 Stepping-Stone

Are you concerned about someone you love who needs a touch from Jesus? Write a prayer to express the need to Jesus. Cast your cares upon Him; as you finish your prayer time, ask the Lord to give you the strength to release the situation to Him in faith.

Jesus replied, *"This sickness is not unto death, but for the glory of God, that the Son of God may be glorified through it"* (John 11:4). Perhaps these words echoed in the hearts of Martha and Mary as they watched their brother being placed in a tomb. Had Jesus waited too long? Gotten sidetracked in His journey? Had He not understood the seriousness of the hour? Would He even come at all? Where was the Lord?

The love of Jesus is displayed in our lives in ways too numerous to count. God's goodness is often underappreciated and overlooked; such precious gifts as raindrops, oxygen, drinking water, the privilege of having choices at mealtime—these are rarely acknowledged as expressions of love from God. However, on the other side of the coin, we can be quick to point out when we see God falling short of our expectations. When we're suffering in an agonizing situation, and we recount the words of request that we prayed to the Father, and then we take into account the limitless power of God, we sometimes struggle to understand how God could love us with unfailing love yet allow us to suffer painful losses. How could Mary and Martha have known as they watched through tear-filled eyes Lazarus's interment that Jesus would soon show up? The devastation from the loss of their brother was magnified by their confusion and disappointment from Jesus's absence. Little did they know, Jesus was completely aware of the timing of Lazarus's death, and Jesus had a plan. Jesus had a cause for His delayed response.

A Quiet Talk with Jesus
Read John 11:17–44 in your Bible.
When Jesus arrived at the outskirts of Bethany, we shouldn't be surprised that it's Martha who struck first to go out to greet Jesus. Martha was always a lady of action! After Martha talked with Jesus, Mary went to meet with the Lord.

Though mourners followed Mary as she approached Jesus, she was able to have a private conversation with the Lord apart from the crowds and from her self-designated "spokesister," Martha. It wasn't enough for Martha to fill Mary in on what Jesus had said; Mary had to hear Jesus's words in her own ears.

When I was a child, I occasionally indulged in playground romance games. More than once, I found myself running to Johnny to tell him that Susie said she liked him, then returning to Susie with news that Johnny was not totally grossed out by thoughts of her. After several round trips, I had delivered enough messages to come dangerously close to getting Susie and Johnny hitched right there under the monkey bars during fourth grade recess. As a child, this method of passing information seemed to be the only appropriate way for two ten-year-olds to communicate, but the back and forth he said, she said would no longer suffice when I entered my adult years. If a young man wanted to tell me something, he didn't dare send his message through someone else. If I was special enough to have his attention, I wanted to hear it directly from him.

You want to hear a love message directly from a sweetheart's lips. It's too personal to involve a third party! Now consider your love relationship with the Lord Jesus. Yes, God speaks to us through a singer's lyrics or through a pastor's message, but are you also approaching the Lord privately on your own to hear His message directly upon your ears?

 Stepping-Stone

Are you content only to hear from God vicariously through others, such as a Bible teacher or pastor, or do you crave a private audience with the Lord? Check off below every method through which God speaks to you. Place a star by the method that you tend to rely upon the most.

- ❏ Sermons
- ❏ Christian songs
- ❏ The words of a friend, teacher, or mentor
- ❏ A written Bible study or devotional
- ❏ Personal study of the Bible
- ❏ Prayer
- ❏ Other: _____

Devotionals and Bible studies are great tools to communicate with God. However, don't miss out on the blessing of allowing God to speak directly to you out of His Word. Read a passage of Scripture. Read it over and over, asking the Holy Spirit to teach you the meaning. Ask God questions if you don't understand. Write down what God speaks into your heart. Pray the Scripture back to God in your own words. Ask God to teach you the discipline of listening in prayer.

When You Have to Walk Through It

Note in John 11:32 that Mary fell down at Jesus's feet. Sound familiar? We earlier found Mary at Jesus's feet in Luke 10:38-42 to listen to His word and grow in her relationship with the Lord. Now we find Mary at Jesus's feet to pour out her sorrows, the act of a woman who was solidly connected to her Master. All who were present must have marveled at the authentic friendship that Mary had with Jesus. What a testimony of Christ's sufficiency, right in the midst of tragedy for Mary!

It didn't seem necessary to Mary that she grieve privately. She knew she could approach the Master, and in fact, Martha told Mary that Jesus had asked to speak with her (John 11:28). She felt welcomed into His presence, though she came broken and with swollen eyes and clouded thinking. Mary said to the Lord the very words that Martha also had expressed to Him: *"Lord, if You had been here, my brother would not have died"* (John 11:32). Perhaps Mary and Martha had said these words to one another over and over as they tried to make sense of the loss of their brother. Mary *knew* Jesus had power over death. But what Mary didn't realize was that Jesus had power over the grave, to raise someone up from the other side of death. Jesus wanted to give her this important bit of knowledge to help build her faith, but it was information best understood through watching the resurrection before her very eyes. To teach Mary this great truth required first that she suffer the loss of her brother.

Did Jesus enjoy Mary's suffering? No. He wept and was troubled. God does take pleasure in watching any of us suffer. But the journey to significant living requires learning and growing, sometimes through relationships with others, sometimes through service, sometimes through reading the Word of God, and yes, sometimes through watching God work through crises. If there is no storm, how can we know that God is sovereign over the storm? If there is no sickness, how can we comprehend Jesus as the Great Physician? How can we point people to the trustworthiness of Christ if we have never experienced His faithfulness through our own personal crisis of belief?

All of us have our own methods of handling loss. Some of us talk it out with people who will listen. Other people refuse to acknowledge the hurt and try to move on with business as usual. Some people are like me; we're retreaters. I tend to want to draw back into myself. I say that I'm sorting through my thoughts, but more accurately I'm replaying the events over and over in my head, I'm trying to make sense of what happened, and I seem to be working toward figuring out who to blame, as though that will bring closure and satisfaction. Sometimes there's no one to blame, and you must cry out to God and wait.

No matter the situation, keep talking to God, and don't forget also to listen. Hold fast to your confession of faith. When you can't muster one positive thing to say about the situation, simply follow the advice of Mary and acknowledge to the Lord that He has all power and authority to do as He wills. God will use your faith in the midst of the crisis as a witness to others, and He will use you as a trumpet to announce His glory and praise at the victorious end of the trial.

Lazarus would probably be cast as the star of this scene, second only to Jesus in this resurrection story, but Mary had a vital role to play. God designed for Mary to take part in this miracle. We can almost imagine the sparkle in Mary's eye and the breathy excitement in Mary's voice as she recounted to scores of people her own sweet version of what happened when Jesus called Lazarus to come forth from the dead.

 Stepping-Stone

Read Ephesians 3:18–19 in the margin. How did Mary's experience in witnessing Lazarus's resurrection help her to better comprehend the love of Christ? How does having spiritual fullness ("the fullness of God") affect your interactions with the lost in your world?

When He Alone Is Pleased
Read Matthew 26:6–13 in your Bible. (Mark 14:3–9 and John 12:1–8 are parallel accounts for further reading.)
Mary's heart was humble, creating within her a quiet gentleness. She had no desire to be in the spotlight. Only an act of worship, an abandonment of self-centered thinking born out of an abiding love for Christ, could usher Mary into the spotlight of attention.

Only days before Jesus's crucifixion, He sat at the table of Simon the Leper. Mary came into her Savior's presence and anointed His head and feet with a pound of very costly spikenard. She let down her hair and wiped the Savior's feet with her hair, releasing her glory at His feet. (First Corinthians 11:15 states that a woman's long hair is a glory to her.) Somehow Mary had a sense of the impending death of Jesus, and her deep adoration compelled her to express her devotion to Him then, *before* He was dead. How could Mary sense that Jesus's death was close at hand when the disciples didn't seem to realize the gravity of the hour? Could it be because Mary listened intently whenever Jesus spoke, allowing her to gain a strong spiritual sensitivity?

I like to imagine Mary as having forethought into this action of pouring out fragrance that would cost a year's worth of wages, but I also can believe that it took every ounce of courage for Mary to express her soul's anguish to Jesus so graphically in the presence of others. The deep love between God and His people compels believers to abandon self in an incredible defiance of prideful flesh.

Once again, sweet Mary drew criticism. Judas was the apparent ringleader of the complaint (John 12:4–5), but the other disciples also spoke out against Mary's extravagant "waste" of the costly fragrance, which could've been sold for a large sum of money and used to minister to the poor.

In 2 Samuel 24:24, King David refused to offer burnt offerings to God using materials that cost him nothing. Does your worship of God cost you anything? Are you sacrificing generously with a glad heart of worship? Apply Mary's example to give extravagantly of herself for Jesus' sake to the call to give of yourself for the sake of the gospel. Do you tend to focus on criticism from others when they see you forsake all for the gospel, or do you look to the ultimate price paid by Jesus on the cross for the cause of drawing all people to Himself, and seek to please Him alone?

Jesus spoke in Mary's defense, approving of her worship. The disciples had a similar mind-set to Martha's, aiming for the practical "do, do, do" of ministry, while Mary was true to character, aiming instead to honor her Savior above all. For Mary, nothing should have been withheld from Jesus, no matter the cost.

Mary acted boldly, but she wasn't the type to thrive on controversy. What gave her the courage to take an action that would place her on the hot seat? Mary was so inclined to be still before Jesus, so in tune to the teachings of Jesus, so sensitive to the heart of Jesus, she was confident the time was right to anoint Him in a lavish act of worship.

If you desire boldness for your journey to significance, take a life lesson from Mary. When God says go and tell, you go and tell, regardless of others' disapproval. Let your sacrifice for Christ be lavish just as your love for Him is extravagant. It's not boldness for the sake of boldness, attempting to prove a point or to be noticed for your courage; it's unashamed confidence that you've heard God's instructions because you have learned from experience to detect His soft whispers. Listen. Listen for God's direction.

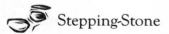 Stepping-Stone

1. Fill in the following blanks:

   [Jesus said,] "And when (the shepherd) brings out his own _____, he goes before them; and the _____ follow him, for they know his _____ ."
   —John 10:4

2. Sometimes other voices compete for your attention. Are there people in your life who desire to lead you where they think you ought to go? How do you respond to their pressure?

3. In your journey to significance, how confident are you right now about identifying the voice of God?
   - ❏ I am certain Jesus is talking to me, and I am listening and obeying.
   - ❏ I am urgently trying to hear from God. I feel frustrated, but I desperately want to hear His voice.
   - ❏ I think I've heard God giving me direction, but I keep second-guessing myself. *(If you checked here, ask yourself if your unsure feelings are because God is asking you to do something you don't really want to do, or to do something that doesn't make "sense," or if it's something else.)*
   - ❏ I can't be sure what is God's voice and what is my own will. I struggle to discern God's will with confidence.

Mary didn't seem to desire a role of leadership, yet she led by example. Jesus told the disciples that what Mary had done would be her legacy, for wherever the Gospel message was preached around the world, the story would be told of Mary's act of worship (Matthew 26:13). Ironically, Matthew and Mark recorded Jesus saying this act would be her legacy yet did *not* name Mary, but in John's account he names Mary but didn't record Jesus's words about her legacy. It's not important that people know our names or recognize our accomplishments. What matters is that Jesus is glorified.

The Fragrance of Christ

On street corners and venders' carts around the world, you can find a wide array of $500 designer pocketbooks, watches, and perfumes for the bargain price of $10 each! Did the vender happen upon a rare opportunity to purchase these items at ridiculously low prices? Uh, no. The pocketbooks and watches look very much like the designer products, but actually they're cheaply made imitations. Don't be surprised when your pretend-Gucci pocketbook begins to unravel at the seams, or your designer perfume starts to repel people who sit too closely! There's no perfect substitution for the real thing.

John 12:3 records that when Mary anointed the head and feet of Jesus, *"the house was filled with the fragrance of the oil."* Her act of worship permeated

Now thanks be to God who always leads us in triumph in Christ, and through us diffuses the fragrance of His knowledge in every place. For we are to God the fragrance of Christ among those who are being saved and among those who are perishing.
—2 Corinthians 2:14–15

the space around her. Now consider 2 Corinthians 2:14–15: *"Now thanks be to God who always leads us in triumph in Christ, and through us diffuses the fragrance of His knowledge in every place. For we are to God the fragrance of Christ among those who are being saved and among those who are perishing."* We are called the fragrance of Christ. Think about what sort of "aroma" you create when you walk into a room—at work, at church, in your home, or in a public place. What words describe what comes forth from your conversations, actions, and carriage? If you're drawing near unto Jesus on a regular basis, you won't emit some cheap imitation of Christlikeness; you will fill the air with the sweet fragrance of the beauty of Jesus, pointing others to the Master. Drawing near to be an authentic witness—it's an essential step in your journey to significance.

 ## Retracing Your Steps to Stay on Course

LIFE LESSON OF MARY: Mary's greatest longing was to be near Jesus.

In light of my use of time, my motives, and my personal priorities, what is currently my greatest longing?

Actions or attitudes I currently employ that are strengthening my resolve to draw near to Jesus:
    1.
    2.
    3.
    4.

Actions or attitudes I want to work toward to strengthen my resolve to draw near to Jesus:
    1.
    2.
    3.
    4.

The greatest obstacle I face in developing a deeper longing to be near Christ is
_____.

To have victory in Jesus over this obstacle, I will _____.

The greatest benefit I can imagine from having a fulfilling, close relationship with Jesus is _____.

Significance Connection: Our witness for Christ begins and is sustained through a growing, vibrant relationship with Jesus Christ.

My willingness to be a witness for Christ will be best sustained by (check all that apply):
- ❑ Obligation
- ❑ Guilt
- ❑ Fear
- ❑ Peer pressure
- ❑ Love for the lost
- ❑ Love for Jesus Christ

Realizing that what Jesus pours into my life is what will eventually pour out of my life, witnessing to others of the power of Christ in me, I will _____

_____

 Stepping Up to the Challenge

Drawing near to Jesus—you've devoted time to studying about it, and now enjoy doing it. Find a quiet space where you won't be tempted to fall asleep and you won't be distracted. Have some fulfilling, quality fellowship with Jesus!

4

Daniel

When They Lose Your Luggage: A Commitment to Godliness

LIFE LESSON OF DANIEL: Daniel's commitment to godliness gained him the opportunity to testify of the one, true God to an entire nation.

SIGNIFICANCE CONNECTION: A lifestyle of godliness will allow the world to see Jesus in the life of a believer, and will result in opportunities for believers to share their faith with others.

Whenever I travel by plane, I get that same anxious feeling. Once the plane has touched down on the runway, I make my way to the baggage claim area. While I'm standing around a motionless conveyer belt waiting for it to start its course, arms folded in a crowd of strangers, a sense of dread sweeps over my mind, and I believe I'm thinking what every other arm-crossed passenger has on his mind: *Did they lose my luggage?* There are many beautiful sights I can name, but one of them is the sight of my luggage making its way around that conveyer belt.

I would like to think if I get to the airport in a timely fashion and clearly label my baggage, it will reach the proper destination when my flight arrives, but that just isn't always the case. For this reason, I try to be prepared by packing my essentials and a change of clothes on my carryon luggage. By committing myself to preparation, my trip isn't spoiled by a glitch that happens outside of my control. Likewise, I would like to think if I try to honor God with all of my heart, my life will go smoothly, but that just isn't always the case either. For this reason, I try to be prepared by growing in my knowledge of God. By committing myself to spiritual preparation, my journey to significance isn't hindered by any opposing force that rises against me outside of my control.

 Focus on You

Chapter 4 of a Bible study is a good time to self-evaluate your daily dedication to becoming spiritually prepared. If you've stayed on track in completing this study, you can speak with experience of the self-discipline necessary to remain committed day by day, but you also can speak of the positive results that come from spending time in God's Word. As you reflect on your experience over the past several days or weeks you have devoted to this study, answer the questions below.

What are the greatest benefits of staying in God's Word each day through a structured, disciplined approach?

What have been your toughest obstacles to staying committed to the Bible study?

After you complete this study, how will you maintain the good habits you've formed while working on *Journey to Significance?*

Enter into a time of prayer, asking God to help you learn a life lesson from Daniel and make the significance connection within your own life.

Resolve of the Heart

Read Daniel 1:1–21 in your Bible.

As I grew up, my family moved often because my dad was in the military. We spent years on the Mason-Dixon line, then in the South, and last in New England. I was young and impressionable, and I tried each culture on for size, but in the end I knew God had fashioned me to be a Southern belle. And now as I travel, people know I'm a Southerner as soon as I open my mouth. You know what they say: you can take the girl out of the South, but you can't take the South out of the girl!

My most difficult transition was in the New England states. The landscape was beautiful and the people wonderful, but I was a young teen during those years, and I certainly did not fit in with the crowd. What had been teens' fad clothing in the South was nowhere close to the teenage styles of the North. The music I had learned to enjoy in Dixie wasn't even available on the radio in New England. My peers had different family cultures than mine, and they longed for different things than I had learned to value. My family stayed for two years, and I never did assimilate into the New England culture. It just wasn't "me."

Becoming a Christian creates an odd reversal of culture shock. Before we receive Christ, we are able to make ourselves at home in the world. We belong to the world. After inviting Jesus into our hearts, we slowly begin to feel a discomfort with the world around us because we're learning to live as Christ. We learn to discern evil and detect our tendencies to worship self, and we withdraw from the very things we used to cling to because we now abhor the reminders of who we used to be. Yes, though we began life fitting in with the world, we slowly progress to being "stick-out-like-a-sore-thumb" Christians who are sojourners and pilgrims in a foreign land that is obviously not our home (1 Peter 2:11).

As you grow in Christ and become less and less like the world, you can feel like a traveler ill equipped to survive this leg of your journey. It's as if you're traveling to your destination, when your travel plans get turned upside down because your luggage gets lost, and you have no earthly possessions to depend upon to meet your needs. How will you survive? How do you live in the world but not operate the way the world operates? How do you respond to temptations and even demands coming from others in authority to make you conform to this world? How can you be prepared? And why does it even matter?

Daniel was ripped from His Jewish home as a young man and swept into Babylonian culture. His training of three years was designed to prepare

Beloved, I beg you as sojourners and pilgrims, abstain from fleshly lusts which war against the soul.
—1 Peter 2:11

him for service in the royal court, and included academic exercises as well as virtual brainwashing to think like a Babylonian. The meaning of a name was significant in some ancient cultures, and Daniel's name change was designed to strip him of his Jewish identity. Daniel went from being known as "God-is-my-judge" to being known as Belteshazzar, or "Bel-protect-his-life."

The key to Daniel's survival is found in Daniel 1:8: *"But Daniel purposed in his heart that he would not defile himself."* He was a man of resolve, and he refused to make compromises with the excuse, "victim of circumstance." If any defilement were to come upon him, it would not be at his hand or within his will. Holiness, then, is a matter of choice. Daniel's environment changed, his name changed, but his identity in the Lord did not change. Therefore, Daniel's manner of honoring God in holy living would not change. And living in a pagan environment, Daniel knew that a conscious decision, a choice of the heart, would be necessary if he were to guard his heart against defilement.

Sometimes it's the little things that get us. An off-color television program here, a lingering daydream of lust there, an occasional indulgence to greed, then the compromise to cheat ever so slightly just this one time—and our resolve has been reduced to paper-thin durability. Daniel's first test of resolve had to do with the small matter of what he would eat and drink. He could have so easily shrugged it off with the excuse of "there was nothing else to eat," or "I didn't have a choice," but he refused to compromise God's standards.

The little things matter in a big way, because integrity tends to jump boundaries. If a man or woman cheats on taxes, that person may one day find it easy enough to cheat on his or her spouse. I remember making a new friend once, and she began to open up and share with me how she used to be friends with several people, all of whom she had become disenchanted with for various reasons. As I listened to my new friend talk, it occurred to me that she would one day also become dissatisfied with me, and I would become one of the many old friends she would complain about to someone else. Of course, that day did indeed eventually come. We tend to follow patterns in our behavior, which made Daniel's choice to address the issue of his meals significant; Daniel didn't realize it, but he was in training for some much more serious temptations to compromise in his future. God was helping Daniel to establish patterns of holiness.

 Stepping-Stone

Beware lest anyone cheat you through philosophy and empty deceit, according to the tradition of men, according to the basic principles of the world, and not according to Christ.
—Colossians 2:8

1. Read Colossians 2:8 in the margin. Name at least three ways you have cheated yourself by following the traditions and principles of the world instead of following God's principles.

2. How was Daniel's choice not to eat the king's meat and drink his wine rewarded by God? How did it affect his witness before the chief of the eunuchs?

3. When you've compromised God's principles in the past, how have you also cheated others around you by not having a strong witness through your actions?

4. Write Malachi 2:2 in the space below.

Holy, undefiled living matters to our relationship with God, and it certainly affects our witness for Christ. Daniel approached the chief of the eunuchs in gentleness, "requesting" that he not be made to defile himself with the king's delicacies. Daniel offered a solution when he presented the problem, and he didn't threaten the chief or make demands of this man who was in authority. God rewarded His peaceful approach and granted Daniel favor with the chief eunuch, who could see there was something remarkably different about Daniel. And after the ten-day test of food, the chief eunuch learned that God was the One blessing Daniel's life. Holy living, in sharp contrast to the world's loose standards, creates a living testimony of the power of God.

Need a Lift?

Read Daniel 2:1–49 in your Bible.

King Nebuchadnezzar was having a crisis of faith. Nightmares plagued him in the night, troubling his spirit so deeply that he was no longer willing to listen to lies. He insisted on the truth. When he called his sorcerers, he must have had doubts about the validity of their "ministry," because he wouldn't give them the opportunity to invent an interpretation by first telling them the dream. In his past, Nebuchadnezzar had been satisfied to play along with the fantastic displays of smoke and mirrors created by the sorcerers, but when his soul got troubled, he refused to play with his religion.

Nebuchadnezzar's spiritual crisis was by God's design. When the people around you experience crisis, start listening to the questions they are asking. God allows difficulties into the lives of people to draw them to Himself, and you, like Daniel, might be the one who will bring answers to their questions.

The sorcerers were dumbfounded by such a tall order from the king. *No one can do what you're asking!* They had no knowledge of the one true God in heaven who reveals secrets (Daniel 2:28). We should never be surprised or enraged when unbelievers make statements displaying their lack of faith, because they live in spiritual darkness. Paul wrote, *"But even if our gospel is veiled, it is veiled to those who are perishing, whose minds the god of this age has blinded, who do not believe, lest the light of the gospel of the glory of Christ, who is the image of God, should shine on them"* (2 Corinthians 4:3–4). However, we who do not live in darkness but who walk in the light of Christ should accept nothing less from ourselves than a strong faith in God that compels us to stand before kings with confidence as we deliver the Word of God.

Arioch, the captain of the king's guard, took a risk by bringing Daniel before the king. If Daniel could not deliver, perhaps the king, who was on a bloody tirade, would have turned on Arioch and his family as well. Daniel must have been in a habit of speaking wisely with those in authority, because we find him once again answering *"with counsel and wisdom"* (Daniel 2:14).

Daniel was a man of prayer, a quality that would later be used against him by evil plotters. He gathered up the other three Hebrew men of the book of Daniel whom we most commonly call Shadrach, Meshach, and Abed-Nego, *"that they might seek mercies from the God of heaven concerning this secret"* (Daniel 2:18). The Hebrew word for "mercies" gives the idea of petitioning God for tender love, compassion, and pity. What an amazing showering of compassion God gave to Daniel! As you read through the dream and interpretation, take note that

King Nebuchadnezzar had a vision that included the everlasting kingdom of Christ (Daniel 2:44), which is even future tense for you and me!

 Stepping-Stone

What qualities have you noticed about Daniel so far that allowed him to prosper under God's authority?

Seizing the Opportunity

Daniel came before the king. This was his great opportunity, perhaps the chance he had been waiting for! To gain special status and a promotion from the king? No, Daniel did rise to a powerful position as a result of the dream interpretation, but it was a rise to greatness that Daniel neither sought nor expected. Daniel seized this opportunity to tell the most influential man he knew, King Nebuchadnezzar, about the one true God. Daniel sprinkled God-talk throughout his speech, and let it be known that he was not able to deliver the message out of his own wisdom (Daniel 2:30). Daniel had been given a God-sized task, but because Daniel brought glory to God instead of himself, King Nebuchadnezzar gave credit to God as well. God once again proved Himself faithful through a life principle that would take Daniel far: *"Humble yourselves in the sight of the Lord, and He will lift you up"* (James 4:10).

Humble yourselves in the sight of the Lord, and He will lift you up.
—James 4:10

 Stepping-Stone

When have you had the occasion to bring glory to God instead of taking credit for yourself? Did the people present acknowledge God's glory shining forth in your life? How could God use such events as bridge builders for future opportunities for you to witness?

When the Truth Hurts

Read Daniel 4:1–27 in your Bible.

It's no fun being the bad guy. I'll deliver flowers; I'll deliver packages; and in a pinch I suppose I could deliver a baby, but please don't ask me to deliver bad news! Do you know those sticky moments when a friend asks if her dress makes her look fat, or if her house smells like kitty litter, or if you think she's ready to sing her first solo, and you suddenly feel the urge to fake a heart attack to get out of telling the truth? How do you suppose Daniel felt about delivering God's message through Nebuchadnezzar's second dream?

King Nebuchadnezzar had a mean streak to say the least, and a tirade from the king usually meant someone was getting cut into pieces or being thrown into blazing furnaces. Daniel would have known about the fury King Nebuchadnezzar had poured out on Shadrach, Meshach, and Abed-Nego when they had refused to worship the golden image (Daniel 3:18–19). King Nebuchadnezzar was not a man who took bad news well.

Do you know any feisty unbelievers? Have you been avoiding telling them the news that they need to repent and accept Jesus as their Savior because you fear their wrath? God loves even mean-spirited unbelievers, and they must hear the truth. God's prophets were constantly delivering bad news followed by good news, and God encouraged them to be bold. We're much like those prophets, delivering the "bad news" to the world that we're all sinners in need of a Savior, followed by the good news that Jesus invites whosoever will to come into the family of God through a relationship with Him. The good news is the solution to the bad news, because God is full of grace. God says, *"Listen to Me, you who know righteousness, you people in whose heart is My law: do not fear the reproach of men, nor be afraid of their insults. I, even I, am He who comforts you. Who are you that you should be afraid of a man who will die, and of the son of a man who will be made like grass? And you forget the Lord your Maker, who stretched out the heavens and laid the foundations of the earth"* (Isaiah 51:7, 12–13).

 Stepping-Stone

How do you approach the aggressive unbelievers in your path?

- ❏ I am not afraid; if they're feisty with me, I just come back with the same measure of aggression.
- ❏ I am not afraid; their souls are more important than my feelings.

❑ I sometimes act like a wilting flower, almost apologetic for my faith.
❑ I haven't approached them about God, because I don't like conflict in my life.

Fear could have been a reason for why Daniel didn't want to tell the king about the horrible fate before him, but Daniel 4:19 makes it more likely that Daniel didn't want to tell it because he cared for Nebuchadnezzar. Daniel had become a loyal and trusted servant to King Nebuchadnezzar. The king respected Daniel as a messenger from God. Daniel took no pleasure in the king's demise, though Nebuchadnezzar had heaped these troubles upon himself by his arrogance and cruelty.

In this incident, Daniel could have given a false interpretation of the dream to spare having to tell the bad news, and King Nebuchadnezzar wouldn't have known the difference. After all, the king's fate was insanity, and he wouldn't have known of Daniel's deception until it was too late. Why did Daniel go forward with the interpretation? Love compelled him. Daniel loved God and would not dishonor Him. But also, Daniel's genuine concern for Nebuchadnezzar led him to tell him the truth and advise the king to repent (Daniel 4:27).

"Therefore, O king, let my advice be acceptable to you; break off your sins by being righteous, and your iniquities by showing mercy to the poor. Perhaps there may be a lengthening of your prosperity."
—Daniel 4:27

Stepping-Stone

Do you tell the truth? Silence is a form of deception and is just as destructive as telling a lie. Practice speaking out about the truth. Read each statement below as if it were spoken by an unbeliever. How could you respond with the truth? Remember, your silence in the face of statements such as these will be received as agreement; tell the truth!

1. "As long as you live right and do right by your family and friends, that's what really matters to God."

2. "People have different ways of worshipping God or relating to God. It just all depends on how you were brought up, I think."

As you read Daniel 5:1–31, you'll find Daniel in another gut-wrenching situation to tell the truth to a powerful and wicked king, and again Daniel didn't back away from the truth. Like King Nebuchadnezzar, King Belshazzar was evil and pagan in all of his ways, yet he recognized the godliness in Daniel (Daniel 5:14).

How did Daniel find the courage to stand before kings to deliver difficult messages? God had proven Himself faithful time and time again to Daniel. Daniel had learned to recognize the patterns of His life by God's design, and he accepted God's plan for his life. Daniel had learned that holiness and obedience bring peace and assurance in the face of trials.

A Living Testimony

Read Daniel 6:1–17 in your Bible.

If people wanted to trap you, what kind of bait should they use? I admit the most effective means for me would be to send a flyer in the mail for a blowout sale on women's shoes, with a valuable coupon attached at the bottom, and the words *free ice cream to the first 100 customers* in bold print across the top of the page. I would walk right into that trap with a big grin on my face.

When Darius the Mede came into power after Belshazzar's sudden death, Daniel once again caused his king to sit up and take notice because of his spirit of excellence and faithful service. The jealous satraps and governors plotted against Daniel, but a moonlight madness sale or an ice cream gimmick wasn't going to work on a man of iron principles. Daniel had been walking carefully with the Lord for too long, and his reputation was solid. How ironic that the satraps and governors trapped Daniel because of his faithfulness to God, and they lured King Darius into the plan by appealing to his prideful ego.

 Stepping-Stone

Read Proverbs 24:10. Daniel likely knew he was under personal attack, and that his cohorts were attempting to catch him in a snare because of his upright living. Place yourself in his shoes, in the day of adversity. Have you ever been singled out negatively because of your faith? How did you respond?

Consistency

When Daniel heard about the decree, note that he went home and prayed from his upper window three times that day, *"as was his custom"* (Daniel 6:10). Daniel wasn't purposing to be defiant, he wasn't exercising his right to pray to prove a point, he was simply carrying on with a pattern that was set into motion years ago. Daniel was being consistent.

Have you ever noticed how we humans tend to buck authority when we feel our rights are being taken from us? If you want a lot of people to read a book, ban the book. If you want a large turnout for your rally, tell people that authorities say they can't assemble to protest. These bursts of response fueled by rebellion tend to be short-lived, as people will go back to their indifference once their rights have been restored. We don't necessarily want to pray, but we don't want to be told that we can't pray. We don't necessarily want to assemble to worship, but we won't stand for being banned from attending church. What backward-thinking creatures we are! Are you already exercising the freedoms given to you by your country? By God?

 Stepping-Stone

1. Daniel's enemies knew they could trap him concerning his relationship with God. On a scale of 1 to 10, how consistent are you 24/7 in your walk with God?

    1   2   3   4   5   6   7   8   9   10

2. Daniel had associated with strong men of God such as Shadrach, Meshach, and Abed-Nego, men who were iron sharpening iron. Read Proverbs 24:21–22. What is the danger to you spiritually to befriend one "given to change"? Are your closest friends strong and consistent in their walk with Christ, or are they given to change?

Now when Daniel knew that the writing was signed, he went home. And in his upper room, with his windows open toward Jerusalem, he knelt down on his knees three times that day, and prayed and gave thanks before his God, as was his custom since early days.
—Daniel 6:10

My son, fear the Lord and the king; do not associate with those given to change; for their calamity will rise suddenly, and who knows the ruin those two can bring?
—Proverbs 24:21–22

3. If America was stripped of her freedoms of religion today, how do you think Americans would respond? Would your daily life have the potential to be radically altered based on your current spiritual habits?

In the Face of a Lion

Daniel 6:10 reveals the content of Daniel's prayers—Daniel was giving thanks to God. Take a moment to place yourself in Daniel's thoughts. Daniel knew his enemies had plotted against him. He realized the lion's den was his fate for praying to God, and that anyone who had watched his daily habits would know that he prayed daily at his upstairs window, facing Jerusalem. Should he have tried to pray in hiding for the 30-day period? No, that would have been fruitless. His enemies were determined to catch him in the act, and trying to hide only would have prolonged the inevitable. Still, would it have been worth a try? Would it have been wrong to hide for his prayertime and hope for the best?

It's a difficult question to answer. Many brave, God-fearing people have been driven into hiding because of their faith. But we can say this with certainty: if Daniel felt no permission from God to pray in private, for him it certainly would have been a sin. Beware of danger when you find yourself praying, "God, I probably shouldn't be doing this right now, but could you please bless and protect me?" Or consider this prayer familiar to some: "God, I am only doing (blank) this one time because of this mess I'm in, but if you will just cover me this one time, I'll never do this again!"

God is not known for blessing disobedience. And though God may not write words on your wall or speak to you audibly, He has a way of making His will known deep in your heart. If you hear yourself thinking, *this probably isn't what God wants of me*, don't do it! As I look back at poor decisions I've made in life, almost always, I knew deep down what God wanted me to do, but I didn't want to admit it because I wanted to do things my way. The most dangerous place to be is *not* in a lion's den under the will of God, but being *anywhere* when you're outside of the will of God.

It is not for us to judge if Daniel would have been justified to hide as Apostle Paul did in Acts 13:23-25, but hiding certainly would have been out of character for a man who had fully relied on the faithfulness of God through the years. This question leads to another factor worth considering.

Daniel was aware of his reputation before the king as well as his enemies. He was known as a man of God, and he was known as a man of prayer. It had been recorded and well reported that Daniel had never compromised his faith in God, not for king's meat and wine, and not from delivering messages of doom in the faces of powerful kings. If Daniel chose to hide his connection to God at this moment in the face of roaring lions, he would have forever damaged the consistent witness he had before kings and men—a witness of the power, the might, the protection of, and the worthiness of the one, true living God. Could he trust his fate to God? God had an impeccable record as Daniel's strong tower of protection. Why should Daniel stop believing God at this stage in his life?

The process of reasoning seems logical enough, but add in a healthy dose of fear and all the imagination could conjure up of the horrible method of death by lions, and it would have taken the peace of God to be as brave as Daniel. How could Daniel be so calm? How could he not devote every word of his prayers to saying, "Please, oh please, dear God, spare me! Don't make me face the lions!" But no, Daniel knelt at his window and breathed prayers of thanksgiving. When I think of what persecution great men and women of faith have faced, I am ashamed of my failure to be thankful every moment of my life.

What an amazing display of grace under pressure! I am certain God gave Daniel the courage to pray unashamedly and the peace to pray with thanksgiving, but let's not fail to recognize that Daniel had been preparing for this moment since he was a teenager. When Daniel landed in Babylon as a young man, he had purposed in his heart that he would live a pure and upright life before his God, and for that reason, Daniel had developed patterns of holiness that kept him consistent. Daniel went home and prayed at his upper window, giving thanks before His God, *"as was his custom since early days"* (Daniel 6:10). If Daniel had compromised as a teenager with the meat and wine, it would have set the pace for a lifetime of compromises.

 Stepping-Stone

1. Think about the last time you felt attacked because of your faith. Did your response to the attack display the trustworthiness of God? Were you tempted to make compromises to protect yourself?

2. My daughter occasionally begs to get permission to do something I have always said no to. "Please, Mommy, just this once?" When she begins to beg, I realize that she doesn't understand why I'm denying her permission. Otherwise, if she understood the action to be harmful or sinful, she wouldn't expect me to give her permission to do it. Place a checkmark beside any of the sins you have ever asked God to cover you for "just this once."

   ❏ Lying to get out of trouble
   ❏ Participating in "party behavior" on a special occasion
   ❏ Blowing off church
   ❏ Withholding your tithe

Why do you think God doesn't grant us permission to be sinful or fainthearted?

3. In Acts 4:18–20, Peter and John express that their zeal for Jesus makes it impossible for them to remain silent about Christ. What about you? Do you err on considering God's mandates as a personal choice, or do you operate in complete resolve to follow Christ?

Special Delivery
Read Daniel 6:18–23 in your Bible.
King Darius loved Daniel, but even greater were the depths of Gof'd love for Daniel as well as King Darius, even more. The Babylonian kings whom Daniel had served had one glaring flaw in common: they all failed to acknowledge

the authority and lordship of God. Note in Daniel 6:14, Darius "was greatly displeased with himself" for unintentionally trapping Daniel, and he worked with all of his heart to deliver Daniel. God would not allow Darius to swoop in and be the hero, because God was going to intervene in this great mess created by Darius's own prideful doing. God was going to be the Deliverer to bring hope where there was no hope. Daniel had something to learn from this lion's den experience, but it wasn't just about him; God allowed Daniel to face this crisis for the sake of King Darius and all who would have eyes to see and ears to hear.

Darius was not a believer, but we might call him a casual seeker. The only recorded words of King Darius at the entry of the lion's den were these: *"Your God, whom you serve continually, He will deliver you"* (Daniel 6:16). Did Darius believe the words he had just spoken? He wanted to believe that God could do what he couldn't, which was to rescue Daniel. Perhaps his utterance was like that of the father who said to Jesus, *"Lord, I believe! Help my unbelief!"* (Mark 9:24).

Darius must have had a hope that God would deliver Daniel, because he showed up at the den of lions the next morning. He cried out, *"Daniel, servant of the living God, has your God, whom you serve continually, been able to deliver you from the lions?"* (Daniel 6:20). Once again, Darius said *"your God,"* not claiming God as his own. Darius evidently didn't doubt God's love, because he didn't ask Daniel if God was *willing* to save him, but Darius did ask if God had been *able*. This moment in history has to be one of the greatest witnessing opportunities of all time! Daniel was found uninjured because he believed in His God (Daniel 6:23), and the testimony that resulted from one man's decision to place his faith in God was broadcast throughout an entire kingdom. Judging from the decree of King Darius in Daniel 6:26-27, the work of God through the life of Daniel had changed the heart of Darius forever. Darius went from decreeing himself as a god (Daniel 6:7-9), to decreeing Daniel's God as the true living God.

 Stepping-Stone

1. Even if you've never been delivered from the mouth of a hungry lion, God has delivered believers from a worse fate—an eternal separation from Him in outer darkness in a horrific place called hell. Rejoice with gladness and tell of His excellent greatness! If someone asked you, "What's so

"Your God, whom you serve continually, He will deliver you."
—Daniel 6:16

I make a decree that in every dominion of my kingdom men must tremble and fear before the God of Daniel. For He is the living God, and steadfast forever; His kingdom is the one which shall not be destroyed, and His dominion shall endure to the end. He delivers and rescues, and He works signs and wonders in heaven and on earth, Who has delivered Daniel from the power of the lions.
—Daniel 6:26–27

great about God? What has God ever done for you?" how would you respond?

2. The Bible doesn't say that Daniel necessarily believed God would spare him, but just that he counted God believable. When you don't know how God is going to work out a situation, what can you be sure to believe about God? Write as many statements of belief as possible. (Examples: I believe God will bring justice to the situation. I believe God cares for me.)

3. Just as your body's muscles are strengthened when you exercise them against resistance (lifting weights), your spiritual muscles are strengthened when you exercise them against an opposing force (moving forward for God despite adversity). Daniel spent a lifetime with his face in the wind, facing resistance and building some incredible spiritual strength. Take a moment and flex your spiritual muscles in the mirror of God: are you getting buff, or are those muscles puny? Are your spiritual muscles growing from repeated struggles against resistance, or do you stay on the path of least resistance?

Daniel's story is not a mandate on God to deliver all who believe in Him from the physical consequences of dangerous situations. Great men and women of faith—John the Baptist, Paul, Stephen, and countless others whose names we do not know—have given their lives for the cause of Christ. It is likely that some time today, a believer in Christ somewhere in the world will either suffer ruthless persecution or will be killed for her faith. Let the words of your Master, Jesus Christ, strengthen you, that you might purpose in your heart that you will not defile yourself for His name's sake. Your persecution will be for His glory. Your opponents must be answered with testimonies about Jesus. Not only the mountaintops but also the valleys of your journey are significant, because your significance is not about your glory—it's about bringing glory to God.

"Behold, I send you out as sheep in the midst of wolves. Therefore be wise as serpents and harmless as doves. But beware of men, for they will deliver you up to councils and scourge you in their synagogues. You will be brought before governors and kings for My sake, as a testimony to them and to the Gentiles. But when they deliver you up, do not worry about how or what you should speak. For it will be given to you in that hour what you should speak; for it is not you who speak, but the Spirit of your Father who speaks in you. Now brother will deliver up brother to death, and a father his child; and children will rise up against parents and cause them to be put to death. And you will be hated by all for My name's sake. But he who endures to the end will be saved. When they persecute you in this city, flee to another. For assuredly, I say to you, you will not have gone through the cities of Israel before the Son of Man comes. A disciple is not above his teacher, nor a servant above his master. It is enough for a disciple that he be like his teacher, and a servant like his master. If they have called the master of the house Beelzebub, how much more will they call those of his household! Therefore do not fear them. For there is nothing covered that will not be revealed, and hidden that will not be known."
Matthew 10:16–26

 Stepping-Stone

1. Fill in the blanks below:

    From now on let no one trouble me, for I bear in my body the _____ of the Lord Jesus.
    —Galatians 6:17

    According to this verse, how is suffering significant in our relationship with Christ? How far are you willing to go in partaking of Christ's sufferings?

2.   Read Acts 20:24 and respond to each phrase.

Nor do I count my life dear to myself...
Who wins when a battle ensues, your flesh or your spirit?

...that I may finish the race with joy...
Describe the joy of spiritual victory.

...and the ministry I received...
Are you motivated to be steadfast as a minister of Christ? How important is it to you that you complete all God intends you to do on your journey to significance?

 Retracing Your Steps to Stay on Course

LIFE LESSON OF DANIEL: Daniel's commitment to godliness gained him the opportunity to testify of the one, true God to an entire nation.

In my desire to have an effective testimony for Christ, I want to purpose in my heart that I will not defile myself with the world's treasures. With the matchless help of God, I want to abandon these worldly trinkets for a lifestyle of holiness:

1.

2.

3.

Bringing glory to God and bringing others to Jesus are more important than these items of worldliness.

SIGNIFICANCE CONNECTION: A lifestyle of godliness will allow the world to see Jesus in the life of a believer, and will result in opportunities for believers to share their faith with others.

I believe that God will create opportunities for me to share my faith when I live as Christ before others. I'm not perfect, but I can be resolved. I want to live by the command of 1 Peter 3:15: *"But sanctify the Lord God in your hearts, and always be ready to give a defense to everyone who asks you a reason for the hope that is in you, with meekness and fear."* I will give some thought and preparation to share my reason for the hope that is within me, which is:

 Stepping Up to the Challenge

If you could write one statement on a banner to have displayed at your funeral, what would you write? What is the life lesson God has taught you? Now consider what statement your family, your friends, your church brothers and sisters in Christ, and your coworkers would write about you. Would each of their statements be consistent? The banners will be similar only if you have been consistent in the way you have lived for God in the sight of others, in public as well as in private.

Record the powerful and succinct life lesson of Daniel's journey to significance, found in Daniel 12:3. In this very verse, you will find the key to being a star, spoken directly from God! Prayerfully approach someone who knows you well, such as your husband or close friend. Ask the person to help you evaluate how consistently you are living for God. Ask your friend to hold you accountable to have a resolve of the heart for godliness, with your goal being to turn many to righteousness.

5

Mary, Mother of Jesus

View from the Backseat: Glorifying Jesus

LIFE LESSON OF MARY: Mary's role in spreading the gospel was found in the shadows of her child, Jesus.

SIGNIFICANCE CONNECTION: A believer's role in spreading the news of Jesus often entails humble "namelessness" in the shadows of the glory of Christ.

Imagine you have been offered the opportunity of a lifetime. A beautiful lighthouse stands tall and proud on the rocky coastline, and you have been asked to be the keeper of the lighthouse. This particular lighthouse is like no other, strategically located in a crucial point of frequent travel, and the warning system of the lighthouse will save countless lives. However, the position of keeper of the lighthouse requires that you remain in the lighthouse at all times. Not only could you never leave the lighthouse, but also no one would ever know your name to be able to appreciate the importance of your efforts. In fact, in all likelihood, no one would even give much thought to the lighthouse keeper, but the lighthouse itself would receive a great deal of attention, because people need the lighthouse. Would you choose this life of sacrifice in order to be a part of the saving of many lives?

Jesus is the Lighthouse, who has come to seek and save those who are lost (Luke 19:10). Rightfully so, all glory, honor, and praise belong to Jesus Christ, the Son of God and Savior of the world. Mary the mother of Jesus was the keeper of the Lighthouse as Jesus was a child, thus playing an important role in God's great plan for the salvation of all mankind. Her life has been celebrated, sometimes well beyond what is appropriate; Jesus was the sinless Son of God, perfect in every way, but Mary was a blessed, God-fearing, obedient *human*, born with a sin nature just like you and me. Mary indeed traversed a journey of significance, but because Jesus was to be in the forefront as her child and also her Savior, Mary's journey required a view from the backseat.

Do you find yourself taking a backseat to the other people in your life? Perhaps you have taken a backseat of importance to your husband, children, boss, parents, or someone else whose life you are pouring yourself into for him or her to succeed in significance. Your life is significant to God, whether God is calling you to be a servant in the backseat or a leader of others in the front seat. Regardless of your station in life, God has called each one of us, not just Mary, to serve in the shadows of Christ. As John the Baptist said, *"He must increase, but I must decrease"* (John 3:30).

 ## Focus on You

Do you like to be onstage with all eyes on you, or do you prefer to recede quietly into the background? Either preference is OK; God has given each of us different personality types to complete various important tasks for His kingdom. But whether you're on the stage or in the background, does Christ shine forth as preeminent? Try to answer these questions honestly in the space below:

- Who makes the decisions for your life?

- Who is glorified in your life?

Enter into a time of prayer, asking God to help you learn a life lesson from Mary and make the significance connection within your own life.

To be Blessed Among Women

Read Luke 1:26–38 in your Bible.

An angel appeared to Mary. Perhaps she would find that disturbing. He seemed to know her, and he knew where to find her. Perhaps Mary would also find that disturbing. The angel said to Mary, *"Rejoice, highly favored one, the Lord is with you; blessed are you among women!"* (Luke 1:28), and according to Luke, *that declaration,* the "saying" of the angel, is what disturbed Mary. Huh? I have read and reread the greeting of the angel, trying to detect what could have been so disturbing to Mary about his words. I admit at times I've been taken aback when someone walks in the room with a greeting such as, "Oh, Kimberly, you wonderful friend, am I glad to see you!" That's because I assume the person is either being sarcastic, or I'm being buttered up to perform a huge favor! In Mary's case, the angel didn't have to flatter Mary with words to get her attention, but Mary felt unworthy of such favored speech directed toward her by a messenger of God.

Flattering words come cheaply from people. Politicians are sometimes accused of "buying" an endorsement from influential people by pledging to push legislation that benefits the flatterer. Wives have influenced their husbands and children have manipulated their parents from the beginning of time through the power of a flattering tongue.

Proverbs 29:5 warns, *"A man who flatters his neighbor spreads a net for his feet."* Why? The Hebrew word in this verse for flatter can refer to a smooth form of speech. When we begin to believe the words of a smooth tongue, we relax our demeanors and we let down the guards of our hearts, leaving ourselves weakened and more likely to walk blindly into a trap of Satan. The flatterer may not have intended to set the trap, but flattery is often initiated with a selfish or deceitful intent.

A person's approval is not what Christians seek. When someone puts her stamp of "OK" on your life, you must have the wisdom to realize that her approval is based upon her own personal standard of what is pleasing and acceptable, making the endorsement of little value. Instead, we seek God's approval.

Do you find it easy to believe flattering words from others? It is not difficult to accept compliments if you've made a quick assessment and believe you are indeed better than the average person! We're taught as children to assess our own personal value in relation to others' abilities. A person is considered rich because he has more money than other people do. A person is intelligent because she knows more information than others. An employee is more valuable when she works harder than her peers.

A man who flatters his neighbor spreads a net for his feet.
—Proverbs 29:5

But we are all like an unclean thing, and all our righteousnesses are like filthy rags; we all fade as a leaf, and our iniquities, like the wind, have taken us away.
—Isaiah 64:6

Thus says the Lord: "Heaven is My throne, and earth is My footstool. Where is the house that you will build Me? And where is the place of My rest? For all those things My hand has made, and all those things exist," says the Lord. "But on this one will I look: on him who is poor and of a contrite spirit, and who trembles at My word."
—Isaiah 66:1–2

God's approval is different. God's favor flows not to the one who has the most, knows the most, or does the most, but instead to the one who honors God Our righteousness is as filthy rags in comparison to God's righteousness (Isaiah 64:6). God cannot be impressed with our great accomplishments, nor does He promise to bless the power-driven overachiever. God has said, *"'Heaven is My throne, and earth is My footstool. Where is the house that you will build Me? And where is the place of My rest? For all those things My hand has made, and all those things exist,' says the Lord. 'But on this one will I look: on him who is poor and of a contrite spirit, and who trembles at My word'"* (Isaiah 66:1–2).

Isaiah had a similar experience to Mary's. In Isaiah 6, Isaiah received the honor of having a vision of God's throne room. As he beheld the glory and holiness of the Most High, he was shaken within his soul. *"Woe is me, for I am undone! Because I am a man of unclean lips, and I dwell in the midst of a people of unclean lips; for my eyes have seen the King, the Lord of hosts"* (v. 5). What a noteworthy progression: the closer we become in our relationship with God, the more we comprehend the holiness of God; the more we comprehend the holiness of God, the more aware we become of the filthiness of our sin. God is fully aware of who we are, the dirt in our hearts, and the blood on our hands, but praise God, He extends His grace to us despite ourselves through the cleansing power of the blood of Jesus Christ. God cleansed Isaiah and then commissioned him to the honor of being a prophet (vv. 6–8). With a humbled heart of gratitude, Isaiah cried, *"Send me"* (v. 8).

 Stepping-Stone

1. Jesus said, *"For whoever exalts himself will be humbled, and he who humbles himself will be exalted"* (Luke 14:11). Consider the following examples of exalting one's self, and place a checkmark beside any that you've been guilty of doing. Write beside that example how to reverse your course of action to exalt God instead.

   ❑ Making sure people give you credit for work you've done
   ❑ Drawing attention to your body
   ❑ Seeking to be the center of attention

❑ Trying to convince people to take your side in a dispute
❑ Sliding information about your accomplishments into conversations
❑ Being motivated to do good works in order to impress a particular person

2. *"All a man's ways seem innocent to him, but motives are weighed by the Lord"* (Proverbs 16:2 NIV). Spend time in prayer, asking God to reveal any impure motives you have in the various ways you are ministering to others in a visible way.

3. Read Isaiah 66:1–2 again. When Mary heard the words of the angel, she was troubled. She trembled at God's Word! Her experience was much like the overwhelming response that Isaiah had when he witnessed the holiness of God. Have you come face to face with God's holiness? Read Isaiah 6:1–8 and ask God to allow you to experience a sense of His glory.

Asking the Right Questions

The angel told Mary she would conceive a child who would be called the Son of the Highest, a king whose kingdom would never end (Luke 1:32–33). Imagine how Mary's mind would've been trying desperately to process all of this overwhelming information! In a matter of seconds her life path had been dramatically altered. Then Mary asked a question.

Notice what Mary did *not* ask. She did *not* ask why. She didn't ask God to justify His plan. This young Jewish girl, whose chastity would have been her only treasure in society, was just told she was going to have a baby, and it wouldn't be from the seed of the man she was betrothed to marry. However, she didn't ask, "Why does this have to involve me?" The old "why me, God?" is a timeless question, one that even Job eventually asked, but we don't hear it out of the mouth of Mary.

Mary also did *not* ask when. We don't like surprises, do we? If a major event is going to take place, we like to be given some prior notice in order to plan and prepare. And wouldn't it have been tempting to say to the angel, "Well, you see, I am willing to do this for God. But there's this wedding ceremony I've been planning for a while now. I sort of already made plans with Joseph. Our family and friends are excited and are really counting on this

"He will be great, and will be called the Son of the Highest; and the Lord God will give Him the throne of His father David. And He will reign over the house of Jacob forever, and of His kingdom there will be no end."
—Luke 1:32–33

as a major event in their lives, and I've had my wedding garment pressed and ready for some time now, and well…could we just postpone this pregnancy until *after* the wedding?"

What we might call the self-centered questions of why or when were not what first popped into Mary's mind. Instead, she asked how this birth could take place in her virgin womb. Note the answer given by the angel: *"The Holy Spirit will come upon you, and the power of the Highest will overshadow you"* (Luke 1:35). How could Mary—a young, innocent, little-educated girl of this particular era, even begin to understand that kind of an answer? But her question was a question of faith. She didn't know *how* it could happen, but she knew that if God was saying it, it was definitely *going* to happen. She didn't have to understand the answer; it was enough to know that there *was* an answer.

 Focus on You

1. Have you been asking God questions about your journey to significance lately? Have the questions been about who, what, when, where, or why? Write down some of the questions you want to ask God about your journey.

2. Sometimes our questions about God's choices for our lives stem from our desire to be in control. Can you relate? When God's hand changes our plans, our flesh can get angry and frustrated, just as Job felt when he lost his family, wealth, and even his personal health. Carefully read the dialog between God and Job as it is written in Job 40:1–14 and 42:1–6, and let God speak directly to your heart. How does Job 42:5–6 relate to Isaiah's throne room experience in Isaiah 6?

Faith-Building Words

Mary received the words of assurance God knew she needed to hear from the angel Gabriel: *"For with God nothing will be impossible"* (Luke 1:37). These were faith-building words for young Mary to cling to in the difficult days ahead. Our God makes a way where there is no way. Think about the implications of how far "nothing" extends—to the cosmos, to the affairs of this world, to science, to your personal life…there are no limitations to God's abilities. Read the following verses aloud and be in awe of the power of the Almighty Living God.

Then God said, "Let there be light"; and there was light.
—Genesis 1:3

But our God is in heaven; He does whatever He pleases.
—Psalm 115:3

Whatever the LORD pleases He does, in heaven and in earth, in the seas and in all deep places.
—Psalm 135:6

"Indeed before the day was, I am He; and there is no one who can deliver out of My hand; I work, and who will reverse it?"
—Isaiah 43:13

He stood and measured the earth; He looked and startled the nations. And the everlasting mountains were scattered, the perpetual hills bowed. His ways are everlasting.
—Habakkuk 3:6

Next Mary took a turn in uttering faith-building words, proclaiming herself the lowliest of servants as a maidservant, and saying, *"Let it be to me"* (Luke 1:38). What an inspiring, courageous statement of release. She relinquished her personal plans for the rest of her life and willingly placed her entire existence into the hands of the Almighty to be His servant. Were they empty words to disguise her true thoughts and feelings? No, for when Elizabeth was filled with the Holy Spirit, she spoke to Mary and said, *"Blessed is she who believed"* (Luke 1:45).

Mary had no way of comprehending what she had agreed to do when she said, *"Let it be to me."* I remember as a young woman saying similar words to God, wanting to give my whole self to God. I didn't know God would give three children to my husband and me to raise when I said those words, and I didn't know about medical hardships I would one day face, and even today I have no idea what difficult challenges are in my future, but I do know of the unchangeable, unfailing ways of God. Because our circumstances do not interfere with God's perfect plans for our lives, we must not allow our circumstances to affect our resolve to faithfully move forward with God, letting it "be unto me."

 Stepping-Stone

1. Do you need some faith-building words of your own? Interact with the words of faith below from Habakkuk 3:17–19, personalizing the phrases to apply to a current difficult situation in your life.

Though the fig tree may not blossom, nor fruit be on the vines...
In your words, "Though I cannot see with my eyes any beginnings of hope for _____
_____
_____..."

Though the labor of the olive may fail, and the fields yield no food...
In your words, "Though I feel like my efforts to _____ are not being successful..."

Though the flock may be cut off from the fold, and there be no herd in the stalls...
In your words, "Though circumstances such as _____ make it seem that things are only getting worse..."

Yet I will rejoice in the Lord, I will joy in the God of my salvation.
In your words, "I choose to have joy in my heart because _____
_____
_____"

The Lord God is my strength; He will make my feet like deer's feet. And He will make me walk on my high hills.
In your words, "I know I can trust God because _____

Though the fig tree may not blossom, nor fruit be on the vines; though the labor of the olive may fail, and the fields yield no food; though the flock may be cut off from the fold, and there be no herd in the stalls— yet I will rejoice in the Lord, I will joy in the God of my salvation. The Lord God is my strength; He will make my feet like deer's feet, and He will make me walk on my high hills.
—Habakkuk 3:17–19

Journey to SIGNIFICANCE

_____
_____
_____
_____.___"

2. List at least three people you know who do not have a relationship with Jesus Christ. Pray with great expectation and hope for their salvation, remembering that nothing is impossible with God.

Chauffeured, but Not Pampered

Read Luke 1:46–49 in your Bible.

The angel Gabriel called Mary *"highly favored one"* and *"blessed"* (Luke 1:28); Elizabeth called her "blessed" twice when she greeted Mary (Luke 1:42, 45). Mary's heart finally burst with joy as she cried out from her very soul to magnify the Lord God. God had noticed her, and He had lifted her up from her lowly state to bless her in a very personal way. *"He who is mighty has done great things for me"* (Luke 1:49). The precious gift of serving as the mother of Jesus is a blessing of God too wonderful to imagine. Tenderly holding the Son of God in your arms to usher His tiny frame to sweet infant sleep, or hearing the first words uttered by the young boy Jesus as He grew beneath your roof would be spectacular. But without in any way minimizing Mary's blessing, could you also say with confidence, "He who is mighty has done great things for me"? Would it take an angel or a close relative or friend to have to point out God's favor in your life, or is your soul already magnifying the Lord?

If *greatness* means God is taking a person places, then yes, Mary achieved greatness. Having Jesus as her child would bring her into an inner circle of intimacy with the Savior, and she would be privy to events that few would be able to experience. Likewise, if you are walking closely with God, then in some way specific to your life, God as the driver is chauffeuring you to greatness, taking you where He wants you to go. But being chauffeured does not mean you will be pampered. What the young mother Mary learned very quickly on her journey to significance was that pain and sacrifice would accompany the blessing and favor of God. Mary had been dealt a difficult assignment.

A Humble Assignment

Read Luke 2:1–7 in your Bible.

When I was pregnant, I would pick and choose those moments when I wanted to be treated normal and when I wanted to be treated pregnant. I didn't like getting unsolicited advice about what I should and shouldn't eat as an expectant mother, or being scolded for lifting an object, but it never hurt my feelings when my husband let me pick a restaurant because of my "delicate stomach" or when my mother insisted on watching the children while I took a nap. OK, I'll admit that I occasionally took advantage of "pregnant woman" status. But there was no such opportunity for poor Mary. The pregnant Mary and Joseph had to travel 80 miles from Nazareth to Bethlehem, translated as "the house of bread," in order for the Bread of Life to be born in Bethlehem as had been prophesied (Micah 5:2).

> *"But you, Bethlehem Ephrathah, though you are little among the thousands of Judah, yet out of you shall come forth to Me the One to be Ruler in Israel, Whose goings forth are from of old, from everlasting."*
> —Micah 5:2

Would you expect at least one stranger to take pity on the young expectant mother, giving up his bed for her to rest comfortably? No special treatment was offered to Mary, and she gave birth to her first child, the promised Messiah, in the residence of livestock. As Mary and Joseph looked upon their holy child resting in a manger and they collected their thoughts, do you suppose they might have wondered if life as the earthly parents of Jesus was always going to be so glamorous? Mary's dreams of precious child-birthing moments were likely ruined. She had no mother or aunt to hold her hand and guide her through it; she was in an unclean environment not well suited for humans, but this was the way God intended it to be, for the Lord of lords to enter the world in the humblest of environments. This time, as well as most times in Mary's future, it simply wasn't about Mary, because it was about Jesus. Mary's life assignment on her journey to significance would always be a humble role, helping to grow the kingdom of God in the shadows of her child.

Stepping-Stone

1. Who would you blame for this terrible inconvenience of having to give birth in a stable?

   ❑ Joseph, for not calling ahead for reservations

   ❑ Your husband's selfish family, the house of David gathered in Bethlehem, for not giving up a bed

   ❑ Your husband's ancestor David, for not being from Nazareth instead

2. Mary endured a humbling hardship to give birth in a stable for the sake of displaying the humble servant's heart of Jesus our Lord. What humbling hardship have you endured as a witness of the true beauty of Christ's servant heart to others?

3. Through the years, Mary had the privilege of learning to have a humble servant's heart by learning from the best example: Jesus Himself. Read the verses below and write a sentence about Jesus's display of humbleness.

John 13:4–5

2 Corinthians 8:9

Philippians 2:7–8

A Public Assignment
Read Luke 2:8–20 in your Bible.

Before I had given birth to a child of my own, I had this image of Mary and Joseph sitting serenely as they gazed upon newborn Jesus, with hay festively spread throughout the stable. Mary had to adjust the fabric wrap about her head, as it had become ruffled during the birthing process. And of course, even though they were in a stable and the period was some two thousand years ago, I always imagined the stable as well lit, warm, dry, and clean. It wasn't until I had made my own visit through labor and delivery that I realized Mary probably was flushed in the face as well as bug-eyed, her clothing drenched in blood and fluids, and Joseph was likely saying a lot of senseless, irritating things while he paced about anxiously with an umbilical cord in his hands. There couldn't have been enough fabric in Bethlehem to help Mary feel clean and dry, nor enough hay in that stable to make Mary feel comfortable. And just when Mary was at her best, in walked a group of unkempt, uninvited shepherds. What a perfect time for company!

[Jesus] rose from supper and laid aside His garments, took a towel and girded Himself. After that, He poured water into a basin and began to wash the disciples' feet, and to wipe them with the towel with which He was girded.
—John 13:4–5

For you know the grace of our Lord Jesus Christ, that though He was rich, yet for your sakes He became poor, that you through His poverty might become rich.
—2 Corinthians 8:9

But made Himself of no reputation, taking the form of a bondservant, and coming in the likeness of men. And being found in appearance as a man, He humbled Himself and became obedient to the point of death, even the death of the cross.
—Philippians 2:7–8

The shepherds weren't there to see Mary; they were compelled to come because of Jesus, yet Mary had to endure the lack of privacy because she was Jesus's mother. This being thrust into the public eye (though Jesus was always the focus of attention) never changed for Mary. Jesus was the center of attention as He preached and performed miracles, but the community also would have carefully observed Mary because she was His mother. When her child died on the cross, Mary had no opportunity to mourn privately or to have one last private conversation with Him. Mary's journey to significance came with the price of losing her privacy.

A Painful Assignment

Read Luke 2:22–35 in your Bible.

Simeon had been waiting for this moment in his life. The Holy Spirit had promised him he would see the Messiah before death. As he prophesied before Mary, Joseph, and the baby Jesus (Luke 2:34–35), he directed his words toward Mary. Did she understand who her child was destined to be? Had the demons trembled at the first cry of Jesus's voice in the stable, at His first breath taken as a babe? And then Simeon made a brief comment that surely penetrated Mary's heart: *"Yes, a sword will pierce through your own soul also"* (v. 35). The word Simeon used for sword meant a large sword. Simeon stood over her 40-day-old baby to pronounce that Jesus would be a controversial figure of history who would endure much suffering, and that she also was destined for continual agony of the soul. Mary's journey to significance would mean great pain for her, drawn out over the life of her child.

 Stepping-Stone

1. Mary needed endurance to complete her assignment. Anything we set out to do, even for God, tends to be increasingly more difficult than when we first began to dream the dream. Read Hebrews 12:1–2, and fill in the blanks.

    Therefore we also, since we are surrounded by so great a cloud of _____, *let us lay aside every* _____, *and the* _____ *which so easily* _____ *us, and let us* _____ *with* _____ *the race that is set before us, looking unto Jesus, the* _____ *and* _____ *of our* _____, *who for the*

Then Simeon blessed them, and said to Mary His mother, "Behold, this Child is destined for the fall and rising of many in Israel, and for a sign which will be spoken against (yes, a sword will pierce through your own soul also), that the thoughts of many hearts may be revealed."
—Luke 2:34–35

Therefore we also, since we are surrounded by so great a cloud of witnesses, let us lay aside every weight, and the sin which so easily ensnares us, and let us run with endurance the race that is set before us, looking unto Jesus, the author and finisher of our faith, who for the joy that was set before Him endured the cross, despising the shame, and has sat down at the right hand of the throne of God.
—Hebrews 12:1–2

_____ *that was set before Him* _____ *the cross, despising the shame, and has sat down at the right hand of the throne of God.*

2. Simeon was able to meet the Messiah before he met death. Simeon was looking for the Christ. Do you know of people in your life who need to meet the Messiah before they meet death? Write their names below. Ask God to work in their hearts, that they may begin to actively look for answers, seeking and finding Christ.

When We Do Not Understand

Mary did not understand how she could give birth to a child since she had never been intimate with a man (Luke 1:34). When the shepherds visited the stable on the night Jesus was born, they probably told Mary and Joseph what they also broadcast throughout the community, which was the message given to them by the angels. Mary surely marveled that angels announced the birth of her child, and she pondered these things in her heart (Luke 2:17–19). When Simeon prophesied about the magnitude of the ministry and reign of Jesus, again Mary was in awe at what monumental events were unfolding within her reach (Luke 2:33). Prophecy was being fulfilled before her eyes as she held the Christ child in her arms. Mary did not understand. Even we who have the Scripture before us, who can read and reread the pages of documentation of the life of Jesus, who can go back and trace the numerous fulfillments of Scripture prophesies and who can read into the future tense of mankind as we study those prophesies which are yet to come, even we sometimes do not understand the ways of God. But not only was Mary struggling to understand the big-picture plan of God, she was a woman just like you and me who was struggling to understand what God expected of her daily and where she was to fit into God's big picture.

Do you struggle with directions on your journey to significance? Sometimes the circumstances around us and the relationships God has placed us in just don't seem to fit together like pieces of a puzzle to give us a clear picture of where God wants us to go. Yet God has said that He is not the author of confusion (1 Corinthians 14:33). When I was a high school math teacher, I taught my students how to solve problems requiring multiple steps. Sometimes the students would get frustrated when we lingered on a particular step, and I would have to remind them: "Just trust me. I'm taking you somewhere. You don't have to understand why we're practicing this step, but you'll know why when we finally get to the end of the bigger problem." When they continued to ask me why we had to do "this stuff," I would reply, "If I explain it to you now, you won't understand. You have to trust me."

To walk the journey to significance for God, we must relinquish control of our situations, and rest in knowing we don't have to make sense of everything happening around us. If we are faithful wherever God has placed us, with eyes and ears open to His call, He will take us where we need to go.

What Is Jesus Doing?
Read Luke 2:41–52 in your Bible.
Imagine Joseph: *OK, Mary, I'll do the talking this time. I can't believe it. Jesus has put us through this ridiculous goose chase for three days! I can't tell you how scared I've been, Mary; how could we explain to God that we'd lost the Messiah? And of all places, Jesus shows up in the temple. Talk about irony. We should have known that was where we'd find Him. What do you think we should say to Him? This certainly is new territory for us, isn't it, Mary? Having to speak harshly to Jesus? Well, He is just a boy. Wait, no, He is more than just a boy.... Mary, I'm confused.*

When Mary and Joseph found young Jesus after searching for three days, Mary's words sounded the same as what any modern-day mother would say to her child who had worried her sick. But the response she received from Jesus was not the stammering and stuttering of a typical child. Jesus spoke with assurance, and Mary and Joseph did not understand. Jesus was standing in the temple as the sinless 12-year-old Son of God. How could they understand? Mary was forced to wrestle continually with theological issues in interacting with her own Son. She was living out the Gospels of the New Testament in her present tense, *before* they were written. Though struggling to wrap her mind around the identity of her child, she persevered for greater knowledge and wisdom. She knew she had a powerful testimony of the Messiah as she stood in the shadows of her child. Are you also willing to dig deeply into the Word of God in order to better understand who Jesus is? Your testimony will strengthen as you gain a better perception of Jesus.

In the Family Circle

Read Mark 3:31–35 in your Bible.

Mary must have felt as if she was on a giant learning curve. For 30 years, she watched her child grow into manhood, and surely the question had run through her mind more than once: *When is Jesus going to start a public ministry?* Once Jesus was baptized and He began to preach and teach, the wheels were in motion and the plan of God rolled full-force right before her eyes. Was she ready for the changes that would have to come? Like any mother, Mary had to let Jesus cut the apron strings when He grew into manhood. But now Mary faced a very different transition: watching Jesus fulfill the role of the promised Messiah. Now Jesus was out of her maternal authority, and he had taken the wheel as the Lord of her life.

Jesus had called His 12 disciples and was now meeting with them in a house, where a multitude had gathered. Jesus's friends were concerned about His behavior and sought to *"lay hold of Him"* (Mark 3:21). As Mary and the half brothers of Jesus arrived, Jesus didn't go with them to offer explanations for His course of action for ministry. Jesus was not being rude to His family; He was drawing a distinction in His role as the Son of God. Though His motivation was pure, the words of Jesus might have stung Mary's ears.

For even His brothers did not believe in Him.
—John 7:5

The multitude informed Jesus, "They're outside seeking You." Note first that Mary and her other sons weren't given any special treatment spiritually because of their earthly relationship with Jesus. They were "outside" the inner circle at that time. Jesus's half brothers weren't believers (John 7:5). Jesus's earthly family would have to accept Jesus as Lord and Savior to become members of the family of God, just like everyone else.

Do you have family members who haven't yet accepted Christ as Savior? Friend, your loved ones need to know and understand that their close relationship with you as a godly woman will earn them no favor with a holy God. Your husband and your children, your mother and your father, your brothers and your sisters, need to know with certainty that a day is coming when they will have to stand before God and give an account for themselves, and you will not be present to speak on their behalf. Yes, they need an advocate, who is Jesus. Only Jesus can stand before the Father on their behalf. Until they have invited Christ into their lives, they are outside seeking Him.

Stepping-Stone

List your family members who are not Christians. Beside each name, list their stated reasons for not accepting Christ as Savior. If you don't know the reason, will you resolve to talk soon to each one personally?

What Does It Take?

Mary had a close relationship with Jesus. She had spent quality time with Him. However, being near to Jesus is not enough. In order to have forgiveness of sins, we must *know* Jesus and be known by Him. Jesus once gave an example to teach this principle: *"When once the Master of the house has risen up and shut the door, and you begin to stand outside and knock at the door, saying, 'Lord, Lord, open for us,' and He will answer and say to you, 'I do not know you, where you are from,' then you will begin to say, 'We ate and drank in Your presence, and You taught in our streets.' But He will say, 'I tell you I do not know you, where you are from. Depart from Me, all you workers of iniquity'"* (Luke 13:25–27).

If these words of the Lord do not sober your soul, read them over and over again. Jesus prophesied that many will seek to enter into Heaven and will not be able (Luke 13:24). These same people will have been present at Bible teachings and church fellowships, and perhaps also will have partaken of the Lord's Supper, but they won't be welcomed into heaven because they will have never entered into a relationship with Jesus Christ as Lord, Savior, and Friend.

Going to church is not enough. Reading the Bible or listening to sermons is not enough. Doing a women's Bible study is not enough. What about being a good person who does good things? Is that what Jesus meant when He said that His family are those who do the will of God (Luke 11:35)? Surely, Mary did countless good works in her lifetime, many acts directly blessing the Lord Jesus, but her good works as the very mother of Jesus were not enough. Consider what Jesus had to say about good works. *"Not everyone who says to Me, 'Lord, Lord,' shall enter the kingdom of heaven, but he who does the will of My Father in heaven. Many will say to Me in that day, 'Lord, Lord, have we not prophesied in Your name, cast out demons in Your name, and done many wonders in Your name?' And then I will declare to them, 'I never knew you; depart from Me, you who practice lawlessness'"* (Matthew 7:21–23).

How can this be? Imagine you are a great fan of a famous author, Jane Famous. You started the Jane Famous fan club; you attend these meetings regularly; you have read her autobiography, written articles about Jane, and have even spent time with some of Jane's friends. You know Jane's family history; you've memorized a few passages from her books; you've gotten people hooked on and excited about her books, and donated to her favorite charities. Then one day you meet Jane Famous face-to-face. You approach her with a warm embrace and begin to ask her about her family. Jane Famous says, "Excuse me, but do I know you?" You proceed to share all you know about her life, how much you admire her work, and all you've done to spread her popularity. However, one crucial fact remains unchanged; Jane Famous looks you in the eye and says, "I'm sorry, but I don't know you. I appreciate that you've done so many things in my name and honor, but that doesn't change the fact that you and I do not have a personal relationship."

What if Mary had only "known" Jesus as a child, but never as a Savior? What if Mary had refused to submit to Jesus as her Savior? What if she had insisted on receiving special treatment, or tried to ignore the "religious" side of her child to maintain the mother/child relationship as she felt comfortable with it? Mary would have suffered the same words falling on her ears at judgment day as Jesus described in these two passages: *"Depart from Me, I never knew you."*

 Stepping-Stone

1. Read Jeremiah 29:11–13. Mary was outside seeking Jesus in Mark 3:31–35. How do we go about a successful search for God?

2. Does Jesus *know* you? Do you have a full assurance that you will be welcomed into heaven? If you have any doubts about where you stand with God, turn now to page 144 to read a summary from Scripture about how to know for sure you've received forgiveness of your sins and will go to heaven when you die.

For I know the thoughts that I think toward you, says the Lord, thoughts of peace and not of evil, to give you a future and a hope. Then you will call upon Me and go and pray to Me, and I will listen to you. And you will seek Me and find Me, when you search for Me with all your heart.
—Jeremiah 29:11–13

God Honors Our Efforts

As her child Jesus, the Sacrificial Lamb of the world, gasped for air while nailed to a cruel cross, Mary had six long hours to reflect on her possible failures as a mother. Her mind probably raced from failure to failure. If she was like most mothers, Jesus probably rolled off the bed at least once as a baby. Mary likely lost her temper with her children from time to time, not because she was undisciplined, but because she was human. It was probably difficult at times to live with someone perfect, and perhaps Mary remembered with great sorrow the many times she had cut her eyes at Jesus. Maybe her mind raced back to the wedding at Cana, when she pressed Jesus to intervene for more wine (John 2:1–12). And now Jesus was being mocked while people spat upon His mutilated body. Perhaps like any mother, Mary had desperate thoughts of what she should have done to come to her child's rescue, but there was nothing she could do.

Helpless. Useless. Incapable. Unworthy. Are you familiar with these emotions? Take comfort in knowing that Jesus was not dwelling on Mary's shortcomings as He suffered on the cross. He was loving Mary, and loving you. *"When Jesus therefore saw His mother, and the disciple whom He loved standing by, He said to His mother, 'Woman, behold your son!' Then He said to the disciple, 'Behold your mother!' And from that hour that disciple took her to his own home"* (John 19:26–27). In His last moments, Jesus honored His mother. If you are a disciple of Jesus Christ, you are in God's family circle! Surely, He will also take care of you.

Transitions

Read Acts 1:12–14 in your Bible.

After Jesus ascended into heaven, Mary's role changed once again. She would forever be known as the mother of the Lord, but He was no longer physically present in her life. Mary had spent the greater part of her life caring for Jesus the Messiah, and now her work was over. Or was it? Mary knew that disciples don't retire until they expire. She continued to serve the Lord, ever to be found in the shadows of her child to the glory of His name. But the transition in her life was tremendous; she went from being caregiver to Jesus to being one of His many disciples.

How well do you embrace change? When the world around you starts to shift, do you retreat into a shell or choose to quit, or are you willing to make adjustments in order to remain effective for the kingdom of God? Life is filled with change. Babies are born; jobs are phased out; ministers move to new churches; people die; hair grays; weight shifts; and the list goes on in an endless series of changes.

God's timing will bring about a series of changes in your life, and God is calling you to faithfulness in each phase. If you lose heart and slacken your pace on your life's journey, you will slow down the progress God has set in motion for you to bring others to Christ. A soul who gives up when hard transitions come is like a beautiful music box that is now winding down; the music fades. You never know just exactly where you are on the track of your race of life, so you must continue believing that around this turn or that, or just over that hill, God will pour out a blessing if you don't lose hope. Galatians 6:9 teaches, *"And let us not grow weary while doing good, for in due season we shall reap if we do not lose heart."*

God said, *"Do not remember the former things, nor consider the things of old. Behold, I will do a new thing, now it shall spring forth; shall you not know it? I will even make a road in the wilderness and rivers in the desert"* (Isaiah 43:19). Let's break this verse down into bite-sized portions for our spiritual nourishment.

Do not remember the former things, nor consider the things of old.
God is not mandating that you forget the past. God often instructed people to build memorials and to recount the blessings He had poured into their lives. If you'll scan back a few verses in Isaiah 43, you'll find God describing Himself in verse 16 as the One who "makes a way in the sea"—an allusion to His past provision to Moses and the Israelites who passed through the Red Sea to escape from Pharaoh (Exodus 14). God is saying, "You haven't seen anything yet! I'm not through performing miracles in your life!" Fight the temptation to dwell on the past. Don't stop at what God did through you at a different stage in life –when you were younger, before you got arthritis, before you had children, before you got divorced, before when you were on fire for the Lord and He used you to witness to others—God is not through using you as a vessel for His mercy until that day when you walk across the finish line of life and breath your last.

Behold, I will do a new thing.
A "new thing" means change! Notice God is doing the new thing; He is inducing the change. It may seem like circumstances are creating a change, or that a heartless person is causing a change in your life, but rest in knowing that sovereign God is in control, and He *is* trustworthy.

And let us not grow weary while doing good, for in due season we shall reap if we do not lose heart.
—Galatians 6:9

"Do not remember the former things, nor consider the things of old. Behold, I will do a new thing, now it shall spring forth; shall you not know it? I will even make a road in the wilderness and rivers in the desert."
—Isaiah 43:18–19

Now it shall spring forth; shall you not know it?
Anything that springs forth seems to come out of nowhere. Will you be looking for God's direction in your life, or will you be consumed in your own thoughts?

I will even make a road in the wilderness and rivers in the desert.
When circumstances try to convince you to lose hope, look to Jesus! With God, nothing is impossible! With God, there is always hope.

 Stepping-Stone

1. Look back into the past ten years of your life. What changes has God made? Write down each major change, and star the ones for which you are most grateful.

2. "Change" is a common concern for everyone. How could you testify of God's faithfulness in your life's transitions to witness to someone who is currently struggling with changes occurring in her life?

Mary the mother of Jesus might be the most celebrated woman in all of history, but she found her contentment in the shadows of Jesus. Some of the greatest unsung heroes of today are men and women who serve as missionaries around the world. Meg Hesch is one of those dear saints of God, and her devotion to Jesus is beautiful. Meg and her husband Roger are missionaries in South Africa. She wrote the following poem and put the words to music as a tribute to the Lord Jesus. Meg is a great spiritual warrior, and she serves namelessly in the shadows of the Savior. To Meg and every other missionary around the globe, and to every person who seeks to serve fearlessly, yet namelessly, that souls may be saved, I say with confidence that your journey is significant.

Empty-Handed

Empty-handed you come to us,
Naked, from the virgin womb;
Glory, power of heaven forsaking,
Laid aside for earthly home.
Mighty Son of God lies helpless,
To our fallen race is born;
Sacrificing all dominion,
Godhead wrapped in human form.

Empty hands are all we bring you,
Nothing worthy in us find.
All our wisdom, pride, possessions,
Transient as chasing wind.
Sinful, we receive Your pardon,
Dying, clasp the Living Vine;
All our hopes in You are hidden,
Jesus, Savior of mankind.

Though I walk in deepening valley,
And my path through suffering lies,
Jesus, You walk here beside me,
Fully human, sympathize.
All my pain and sorrows bearing,
Lift me from the mire of sin;
Jesus, you came down from heaven,
So that heaven I might win.

Now exalted in the highest,
Name above all names the best,
Your glory radiant in our faces
As we keep Your Advent feast.
God's purpose formed before the ages—
Eternity in us to dwell—
Now lives in us, our great Redeemer,
Jesus, our Emmanuel!

Stars and angels sing around You,
Shepherds the glad tidings tell,
Wise men worship and adore you,
Jesus our Emmanuel!

—Meg Hesch, December 2006

Retracing Your Steps to Stay on Course

LIFE LESSON OF MARY: Mary's role in spreading the gospel was found in the shadows of her child.

In order to spread the good news of Jesus Christ to the world around me, I am willing to submit to God as a humble servant. In my desire to be a living testimony of God's trustworthiness, I will bring glory to God instead of pleasing myself by doing the following:

1. At home:

2. At church:

3. At work:

4. In my other friendships:

SIGNIFICANCE CONNECTION: A believer's role in spreading the news of Jesus often entails humble "namelessness" in the shadows of the glory of Christ.

I don't have to be recognized by my peers for the work I do for the Lord because _____

_____

_____ .

_____

_____ .

_____

_____ .

_____

_____ .

_____

_____ .

While my name is not eternally significant, the name of Jesus is. Because I want to love people as much as God does, I want to use creative ways to bring the name *Jesus* before the lost who are in my sphere of influence. With God's help, I can bring the name of *Jesus* to the attention of others by using these creative ideas:

1.

2.

3.

4.

 Stepping Up to the Challenge

Jesus is your greatest example of how to deny the temptation to glorify self in order to glorify the Father in heaven. What was Jesus's motivation to remain committed to a life of humble servanthood? Record Jesus's words found in Matthew 20:28 on an index card. Meditate on Jesus's words each day for a week and commit this verse to memory. Ask God to reveal to you how you can give your life as a means for many to come to salvation in Jesus Christ.

6

Esther

No Time to Sightsee: Having an Impact on Your World

Life Lesson of Esther: Esther chose to abandon her place of comfort and safety for the sake of the lives of others, embracing the divine appointment God had scheduled for her.

Significance Connection: God is calling believers to abandon their self-made places of comfort and safety to get personally involved in the lives of others, embracing the principle that God intersects believers with unbelievers that the gospel might spread.

But when the fullness of the time had come, God sent forth His Son, born of a woman, born under the law, to redeem those who were under the law, that we might receive the adoption as sons.
—Galatians 4:4–5

My middle child and I have something significant in common: we're both adopted. Jay came into our home from Guatemala when he was seven months old, and he is a very loved, cherished, and honored member of our family. I can't be certain what life would have been like for Jay if he hadn't been adopted, but he likely was rescued from a life of poverty with little hope to escape a desperate situation.

I was raised in a loving, godly home with my biological parents, but I have been spiritually adopted by God (Galatians 4:5). I entered into the family of God when I became a Christian at the age of 7, and I am a very loved, cherished, and honored member of God's family (Exodus 19:5; Romans 9:25). I can't be certain what life would have been like for me if I hadn't been spiritually adopted into God's family, but I was unquestionably rescued from great spiritual poverty, complete separation from God, and the guilt of sin, with no hope to escape my desperate situation apart from Jesus Christ.

Sometimes an adopted child will reach a stage as he grows when he asks himself, "Why was I selected by my adopted parents to be in their family?" Sometimes I also ask myself, "Why me? Why has God chosen such a wretched person like me to be His child?" Jesus said, *"You did not choose me, but I chose you"* (John 15:16). He also said, *"For everyone to whom much is given, from him much will be required"* (Luke 12:48). God has chosen me to serve Him not just for my own pleasure, but to fulfill a greater purpose for my life.

In this chapter, you will be studying the life of Queen Esther, who might have said, "Being a queen would be easy if I didn't have any responsibilities to God or my people." Her royal marriage ushered her to a position to face dangerous opposition from the very beginning of her reign. Queen Esther had been given the world at her fingertips by a man who wished nothing more for her than that she look beautiful and enjoy each day like it was a vacation, but Esther learned quickly, there was no time to sightsee on her journey to significance.

What about you? What has God purposed for you to do? Are you doing it? And are you enjoying the privileges of being a child of God through spiritual adoption? Looking beyond the difficulties of life to draw strength from the joy of your salvation takes discipline.

 Focus on You

Complete one or all of the following sentences:

Marriage would be easy if

Having a job would be easy if

Raising children would be easy if

Enter into a time of prayer, asking God to help you learn a life lesson from Esther, in order that you can make the significance connection in your life.

Rising Without a Name

Read Esther 1:1 through 2:18 in your Bible.

Esther is one of only two women with a book named after her in the Bible (the other being Ruth). Her name appears more frequently than any other woman in the Bible, with 55 occurrences. Esther is famous as a woman of Scripture, but Esther began as a nameless, orphaned Jewish girl reared by her cousin Mordecai.

Many famous heroes had humble roots. Jesus, the Hero above all heroes, was not a nobleman's child, but was raised in a carpenter's family. There's a pervading belief today that poor status in childhood is a contributing factor, if not a determining factor, for failure into adulthood, but those experts who write the headlines fail to remember that *"with God, nothing will be impossible"* (Luke 1:37). God is not hindered by circumstances; in fact, His glory shines quite beautifully when He pulls a struggling soul from humble circumstances and positions her for greatness.

Have you ever blamed your past for your present failures, or felt limited by your circumstances? Do you think less of yourself because of your humble lifestyle or beginnings? The solution to overcoming these negative thoughts is biblical, but it goes very much against the formulas for "positive thinking" found in self-help books. It's not that you must learn to think much of yourself, to value your self-worth, or to believe in what you can achieve; instead, you simply must learn to believe God. God has called you a precious treasure (Exodus 19:5). He says you are a conqueror (Romans 8:37). God has declared you righteous (Philippians 3:9), and He has commissioned you to the high calling of serving as His ambassador (2 Corinthians 5:20). If you are a Christian, you have been declared a child of God (John 1:12), you are thoroughly equipped for every good work (2 Timothy 2:21), and God has a plan for you to be prosperous (Jeremiah 29:11–13). God has described you in a positive light in all of these ways and many more. Do you believe God? Will you allow Him to define you, or will you choose to allow society to define you? Will you allow God to determine your abilities and limitations, or will you let your circumstances determine your abilities and limitations?

Not having my own righteousness, which is from the law, but that which is through faith in Christ, the righteousness which is from God by faith.
—Philippians 3:9

Now then, we are ambassadors for Christ, as though God were pleading through us: we implore you on Christ's behalf, be reconciled to God.
—2 Corinthians 5:20

But as many as received Him, to them He gave the right to become children of God, to those who believe in His name.
—John 1:12

Therefore if anyone cleanses himself from the latter, he will be a vessel for honor, sanctified and useful for the Master, prepared for every good work.
—2 Timothy 2:21

For I know the thoughts that I think toward you, says the Lord, thoughts of peace and not of evil, to give you a future and a hope. Then you will call upon Me and go and pray to Me, and I will listen to you. And you will seek Me and find Me, when you search for Me with all your heart.
—Jeremiah 29:11–13

 Stepping-Stone

1. What are some of the challenges of your past or present that could interfere with your success in the future? List them below, then underline the ones you are allowing to limit what God would do for you and through you for the sake of the kingdom of God.

2. Think about the women around you who are struggling with their self-image and are lost without Christ. How can you share these words in bold listed in the previous paragraph with a hurting woman to teach her what God is offering her through Jesus Christ?

Beyond Her Beauty

Esther had a few important chips stacked in her favor. She was a young woman with a doting adoptive parent in Mordecai (2:7, 11). She had a strong family heritage (2:5–6). Apparently Esther also had learned a valuable life lesson at a young age, which was to heed the wisdom of those in authority over her (2:10, 15). Furthermore, bless Esther's heart, God gave her the gift of beauty. King Ahasuerus (or Xerses [ZURK-seez]) had appointed officers in each province of his kingdom to collect virgin women with only one special quality: physical beauty. Esther was selected to be a member of this elite group of women who would receive a year of beauty treatments at the royal palace under the supervision of Hegai the eunuch. In her own community, she was surely a standout beauty, but once in the palace, she was in a sea of beautiful faces. How, then, did she gain favor with Hegai and with the king?

Consider what King Ahasuerus *didn't* want in a wife. Queen Vashti was such a beautiful woman that King Ahasuerus, the kind of man who would hold a 180-day feast in order to flaunt his wealth, wanted to put her on display before the people and the officials. Her refusal to obey his command made her no less physically beautiful, but it did place an ugly scar on the king's appearance in the eyes of his people. Gender roles were significant in their culture, and Vashti's defiance was taken so seriously by the king's inner circle of advisors that they were expecting kingdom-wide ripples of household mutiny (1:17–18)!

Memucan suggested that King Ahasuerus find someone "better" than Vashti (1:19). Did he mean better looking? No, Vashti was already a dazzling beauty queen. Memucan wanted the king to have a royal wife who would honor his manhood and his kingship, and thus set an example for other women in the kingdom. When King Ahasuerus sent out the call for a new bride, he was ultimately looking for more than a pretty face.

King Ahasuerus and even the king's eunuch, Hegai, were surrounded by many beautiful women. Sexual manipulation would be of little use to gain favor with either man, a cheap ploy that many of the young virgins would have attempted, no doubt. No, there was something attractive about the character of Esther that made Hegai want to help Esther succeed and made King Ahasuerus want to place a crown on her head. I somehow imagine, though the Scripture gives no explicit details about Esther's demeanor, that God's favor rested upon Esther in a most appealing way to the outsider because of Esther's humble words and deeds.

 Stepping-Stone

Read 1 Peter 3:1–4.

1. In verses 1–2, is the emphasis on the words or conduct of a wife?

2. In verse 4, Peter says to adorn ourselves with the *"hidden person of the heart."* How often do you allow your spouse to see that beautiful person hidden within you? What hinders you from exposing your inner beauty more often? (Do you fear being vulnerable? Are you too busy? Do you feel unattractive?)

Wives, likewise, be submissive to your own husbands, that even if some do not obey the word, they, without a word, may be won by the conduct of their wives, when they observe your chaste conduct accompanied by fear. Do not let your adornment be merely outward—arranging the hair, wearing gold, or putting on fine apparel— rather let it be the hidden person of the heart, with the incorruptible beauty of a gentle and quiet spirit, which is very precious in the sight of God.
—1 Peter 3:1–4

3. According to verse 4, what attributes of a woman's spirit are beautiful in the sight of God?

4. *Quiet* in verse 4 is the Greek word *hesuchios*, which carries nuances of being "undisturbed" and "undisturbing." What do you allow to disturb your mood, and how does that affect your interactions with your husband and others? Do you have a tendency to stir up disruption in the lives of others? How does your mood affect your witness?

5. Esther chose to heed Mordecai's command not to reveal her Jewish heritage (2:10). Do you conceal your Christian identity for fear of rejection by your spouse? Your friends? Your coworkers?

The Hands-Off Approach

Read Esther 3:8 through 4:4 in your Bible.

Esther had little time to enjoy being queen before she had to assist Mordecai in thwarting an assassination attempt on her husband's life (Esther 2:19–23). Then Haman officially wrecked the honeymoon: by his suggestion, a decree had been signed, sealed, and delivered for the annihilation of the Jewish people in Persia in exactly eleven months. The Persian Jews, including Mordecai, were mourning with deep emotion and sackcloth on their backs. Word had reached Queen Esther that Mordecai was in sackcloth before the king's gate. What would be the appropriate response?

As Christians, we know God has called us to reach out to others in need, thus we must determine how to respond when those needs come to our attention. Some of the potential responses require hands-on ministry, like sitting with a sick friend, driving a neighbor to work, or taking Bibles into a rough neighborhood. Hands-on means sacrificing time, adjusting our personal schedules, making room in our hearts to love the unlovable, and resolving to do whatever it takes to meet others' needs.

However, the hands-off approach creates far fewer ripples in our daily agendas. If we are willing to send food, write a check, or pronounce a well-wish, should that not count for something? It pained Esther to think of Mordecai in distress. Her response? She sent fresh garments to replace his outward expressions of sorrow. We could think of it as sort of a "don't worry, it will be OK" pick-me-up bouquet. She didn't inquire about the problem creating his sorrow, but instead sent an expression of love and concern that required no sacrifice or involvement on her part. Mordecai rejected the garments, perhaps feeling insulted by her shallow sympathy. Those fine garments could bring no relief to Mordecai's grieving heart.

 Stepping-Stone

1. Think about Esther's gesture of concern by sending the garments. Did her gesture do any of the following?

   Honor Mordecai.

   Come at great cost to Esther.

   Require personal sacrifice of Esther.

   Express a willingness to get involved.

   Relate a deep understanding or appreciation for Mordecai's sorrow.

2. When a friend is hurting, do you tend to jump in to help with compassion to the point of personal sacrifice, or do you tend to offer more surface responses? What about the pain of a stranger?

Compassion for the Body, Compassion for the Soul

It was bitterly cold outside, the kind of weather that makes you crave chili. As I stood in line at the fast-food counter, a dirty man with matted hair and ragged clothes entered the restaurant. I'm sure I stared at him, though I never meant to. He made his way to the clerk, and with eyes cast low, he spoke in a small voice to beg humbly for food. The clerk nervously shifted, looking at the ceiling and turning down his request time and again as he continued in a hushed tone to plead for something he obviously needed badly. Tears filled my eyes as I heard God whisper in my ear, *When you have done it unto one of the least of these, you have done it unto Me.*

I stepped up to the counter and insisted I would pay for whatever he wanted, and then it was my turn to beg as I pleaded with the man to take more than what he had ordered. He kept his eyes to the floor throughout the entire awkward scene, except for one brief and very powerful moment, when he turned his face toward mine, locking eyes with me, and said, "Thank you." He took his tray and quietly slipped into a dark corner to eat his food in silence.

My heart was filled with pity as I pulled out the few dollars and cents, and I soon sat down with my friend at a booth with the meal that we had ordered. As my eyes refused to stop gazing over at the homeless man's table, I nearly choked on my food as I thought about what I *hadn't* done for the man. It was easy to pay a small bill for a hungry man to eat, but that very night he would be on the streets with no defense against a bitter cold that would overcome his shell, much like the confusion and lostness that had overcome his heart. He needed a friend, but I never even asked his name. He needed compassion, but I never asked him his story. He needed encouragement, but I never told him my story. He needed Jesus, but I never spoke of His name.

I met a man who was lonely, desperate, and hurting, and I bought him a sandwich and sent him on his way. I daily feast at the banquet table my Lord provides for me, yet I walked away from a man who was spiritually starving and I never told him about God's provision already made for him. I was hands-off, and that man was no better for ever having met me. The hands-off approach was as much to my detriment as it was to his.

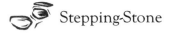 Stepping-Stone

1. You know people in your sphere of influence who are needy. Some are physically needy, and many are spiritually needy. On the scale below, mark your level of involvement in the lives of those around you who are needy.

Physically Needy
❑ I don't ask what's going on because I don't want to know.
❑ I listen to their problems, but I don't respond.
❑ I let them know I'll pray for them.
❑ I pray for them and try to help as I am able.
❑ I have surrendered to do whatever it takes to help others.

Spiritually Needy
❑ I don't ask what's going on because I don't want to know.
❑ I listen to their problems, but I don't respond.
❑ I let them know I'll pray for them.
❑ I pray for them and try to offer godly wisdom.
❑ I have surrendered to sharing Christ with them as often as God prompts me to share.

2. Read 1 Thessalonians 2:8. Paul was willing not only to share the gospel, but also to share his _____.

So, affectionately longing for you, we were well pleased to impart to you not only the gospel of God, but also our own lives, because you had become dear to us.
—1 Thessalonians 2:8

- How would your life be affected if you were to share your life along with the gospel with the unbelievers in your sphere of influence? What changes would you have to make? What would be the rewards for making this choice? What hinders you from making this choice?

- Paul was willing to share his life with them because they had become dear to him. Write a prayer in the space provided at the top of page 134, asking God to give you such a deep love for the lost people in your life that you would feel compelled to share your life with them.

Facing Unpleasant Responsibilities

Read Esther 4:5–11 in your Bible.

When Mordecai refused the clothing from Esther, her heart was stirred to intersect with Mordecai's pain. She sent the eunuch Hathach to gather details from Mordecai, and Mordecai did what so many of us fear will happen when we open ourselves up to the hurting—Mordecai not only informed her of the problem, but he asked her to be a part of the solution. Mordecai asked her to go before the king to plead for her people.

Interceding for others can be tricky. It feels so much like interfering, and it's generally a tightrope walk of words. Esther was surely sympathetic to Mordecai's plea, but I can imagine her mind racing immediately to invent another solution, a plan B, to save her people. She hadn't been summoned, and entering her husband's inner court without invitation was punishable by death unless the king extended his golden scepter. In the process of attempting to save her people, it was very possible that she herself would be put to death if she went before the king.

Upon hearing Mordecai's command for her to plead with the king, her reply was basically, "It's not that easy. You don't realize what you're asking me to do!" Take a moment for self-examination. Once you open your heart to serve God, He brings to your attention those around you who are wounded and weary, and He invites you to attend to their needs as the hands and feet of Christ. Now suddenly you also are in crisis, for serving as Christ requires personal sacrifice and abandonment of comforts. You might think to yourself, *I'm sympathetic to their sorrows, but I am not in a position to do something about it.* You begin to count the costs and identify what you would lose in order for the other person to gain. Perhaps a crisis of belief sets in, as you question with great hopefulness if maybe God hadn't really asked you to get involved after all, because He's sending someone else who is in a better position to help.

It's not pretty, is it, when you come face to face with your thoughts, the thinking that you don't want to identify with but which most accurately defines your walk with Christ? It's the old adage put to the test: will you walk the talk? I'm ashamed to count how many times I have been like the priest or the Levite, who saw the wounded soul lying helpless in the ditch, and with a self-important excuse I passed him by (Luke 10:30–37).

Intersecting with people's lives for the glory of God can be messy business. Seeking first the kingdom of God is going to require involvement with people, and people have problems. Many are unwilling to receive help, and others are far too willing to let you tackle all of their problems for them. People have immediate needs, and they often have spiritual needs that they aren't even aware of themselves. People can be ungrateful, and they can stretch you to the limit. Perhaps that's why so many Christians take an early retirement from church work, and why many churches can't get nursery workers! Kingdom work also can be hazardous. Christians worldwide have lost their lives, lost their jobs, lost their friends and family, and suffered persecution like we've never known for the cause of Christ. It's a simple truth all Christians must face: serving Jesus will cost you something.

When we put the needs of others before our own personal safety and comfort, we are like Christ, the Sacrificial Lamb. What did He have to say to believers about facing adversity for His sake? Read Matthew 10:27–31 in the margin to see what Jesus instructs us to do.

- **Proclaim my message boldly** (v. 27). Be visible when we speak up for Christ, and position ourselves to be heard by the world.
- **Fear God more than you fear humans** (v. 28). What a heartbreaking truth: when we are silenced by fear of how others might harm us because of our faith, we are more concerned with pleasing evil people than a Holy God. Are we more fearful of the consequences rendered by humans than the consequences rendered by God? (Read 2 Corinthians 5:10–11 in the margin concerning consequences rendered by God's hand.)
- **God is fully aware and in control** (vv. 29–30). Not even a small incident in nature is beyond God's watchful eye. What a great reminder to us that God cares for us very specifically. When we feel small and unimportant, we can recall with great joy that we are VIP's in God's kingdom, and He is engaged with every detail of our lives. We matter to God.
- **Because He is able and willing to help you, do not fear** (v. 31). If such thinking came naturally, Jesus wouldn't have had to teach this lesson to the apostles. This passage comes on the heels of Jesus sending out the Twelve, warning them of persecutions to come. Jesus has sent us,

"Whatever I tell you in the dark, speak in the light; and what you hear in the ear, preach on the housetops. And do not fear those who kill the body but cannot kill the soul. But rather fear Him who is able to destroy both soul and body in hell. Are not two sparrows sold for a copper coin? And not one of them falls to the ground apart from your Father's will. But the very hairs of your head are all numbered. Do not fear therefore; you are of more value than many sparrows."
—Matthew 10:27–31

For we must all appear before the judgment seat of Christ, that each one may receive the things done in the body, according to what he has done, whether good or bad. Knowing, therefore, the terror of the Lord, we persuade men; but we are well known to God, and I also trust are well known in your consciences.
—2 Corinthians 5:10–11

and He sends us with a full awareness that we may be persecuted for His name's sake. He has given us these words of encouragement in Matthew 10:27–31, and now Jesus issues this sobering conclusion: *"Therefore whoever confesses Me before men, him I will also confess before My Father who is in heaven. But whoever denies Me before men, him I will also deny before My Father who is in heaven"* (Matthew 10:32–33).

What will it take for you to abandon your fears for the sake of Christ? What did it take for Jonah? (Tag: Suggest adding Scripture references for this and Peter, following a very juicy and smelly three-day time-out in the belly of a fish. What about Peter? He was subjected to the reality of his feeble faith when he denied Jesus three times in His hour of need. Beg God for courage to overcome, that there might be no more time-outs and no more denials of Christ in your journey to significance.

 Stepping-Stone

1. What are the lengths you are willing to go to for the cause of Christ? Assess your spiritual courage on a scale of 1 to 10.

2. Name three things you have chosen *not* to do for Christ because you feared the consequences.

    1.

    2.

    3.

3. What is the furthest extent you have ever gone for Christ, pushing through danger or pain? How did you find the courage to do it? What were the results?

4. Read Luke 10:25–37, the story of the Good Samaritan. If you are to follow Jesus's instructions in verse 27, can you choose to opt out of obeying God when the cost to you is great? Have a prayertime with God, letting Jesus repeat to you His words spoken in verse 37, speaking of mercy: *"Go and do likewise."* Ask God to get specific with you about how to show mercy to others today. You can note later what He does in this space provided.

For Such a Time as This
Read Esther 4:12–17 in your Bible.

I am famous for making plans. I plan all of my family's vacations. I plan conferences and women's retreats. Even when I'm not officially in charge, I still am inclined to make plans. My planning tends to be thorough and completed well ahead of schedule. For instance, though today held a record-breaking heat wave for August, I sat down this evening after supper and looked over my Christmas gift list. My plans don't always succeed, but one thing is true: I never plan to put myself in an uncomfortable situation. In fact, I love making plans because they help me *not* to be caught off guard with a difficult challenge.

God is also famous for making plans, and His plans always prevail. The psalmist wrote, *"Your eyes saw my substance, being yet unformed. And in Your book they all were written, the days fashioned for me, when as yet there were none of them"* (Psalm 139:16). God spoke through Jeremiah, *"For I know the thoughts that I think toward you, says the Lord, thoughts of peace and not of evil, to give you a future and a hope"* (Jeremiah 29:11). God's plans for your life have an eternal essence about them, and those plans are in every way meant ultimately to give you an amazingly blessed future.

However, within all of these assuring words from God, nowhere does God promise to shelter you from hardship. In God's divine plan for your life, hardships and personal challenges are scattered along your journey to significance, all intended to strengthen you, bless others, and bring glory to the kingdom of God. When you find yourself in a position such as Esther, asked to step into danger for a worthy cause, be assured as you go in God's will that you were made for such a time as this.

Your eyes saw my substance, being yet unformed. And in Your book they all were written, the days fashioned for me, when as yet there were none of them.
—Psalm 139:16

For I know the thoughts that I think toward you, says the Lord, thoughts of peace and not of evil, to give you a future and a hope.
—Jeremiah 29:11

Young Esther was focused on self-preservation, but with every Persian Jew about to perish by the sword, Mordecai had no time to sugarcoat his words for Esther's delicate ears. Note his amazing perception in his first words back to Esther: *"Do not think in your heart..."* (2:13). Dear sister, your thoughts are extremely powerful. As odd as it sounds, try to *think* about your thoughts. When you are faced with decisions about helping others, serving God, being obedient, fighting temptation, or any other spiritual matter, your mind is debating very personal beliefs. Much of what you think, you would never say out loud to others, nor would you want to acknowledge those thoughts to yourself. Mordecai was expressing to Esther, *Don't fool yourself.*

I catch myself being so foolish at times. I remember once debating in my mind if I wanted to talk to God about a particular matter, because I knew if I brought it up to God, I would have to acknowledge I had felt the Holy Spirit nudging me to do something difficult, and then God would very pointedly ask me to do what I wasn't sure I was willing to do. As the debate raged on while I sat on my prayer stool, it hit me: God knows my thoughts! Silly me, the secret was already out! I couldn't hide anything from God, and God was in control whether I wanted to acknowledge it or not. I had caught myself *thinking in my heart.*

 Stepping-Stone

1. Mordecai sensed selfishness in Esther's response to his plea for help. Where do you need selfishness rooted out in your personal life?
   ❏ Your marriage
   ❏ Your finances
   ❏ Your "free" time
   ❏ Your desire for recognition or fame
   ❏ Other: _____

2. Selfishness is a characteristic that can remain hidden under the surface until someone needs something you have. Read Proverbs 11:26. What do you have to offer those around you who are in need?

The people will curse him who withholds grain, but blessing will be on the head of him who sells it.
—Proverbs 11:26

Journey to SIGNIFICANCE

3. As you read this chapter and confront your level of self-preservation versus self-sacrifice for the sake of others, what are you *thinking in your heart*? Ask God to reveal these thoughts, and write them down as plainly as possible.

The Right Place at the Right Time

In my Bible study, *Journey to Confidence: Becoming Women Who Witness*, I talk about an important life principle based on Acts 17:26–27: "*And He has made from one blood every nation of men to dwell on all the face of the earth, and has determined their preappointed times and the boundaries of their dwellings, so that they should seek the Lord, in the hope that they might grope for Him and find Him, though He is not far from each one of us.*" Esther's life is a perfect example of this principle, which simply states that God places each person in the right place during the right time in order for each of us to seek Him and find Him. God had placed Esther in the right place at the right time to rise to a powerful position as queen to King Ahasuerus. Why did Ahasuerus want her to be the queen? Because she was a beautiful and pleasant young woman. Why did God want her to be the queen? For an entirely different reason: so that she would seek His help and draw close to Him as the refuge and strength for her and her people. She was in the right place at the right time with the right connections to make a significant difference for the people of God. But in the heat of the moment at this critical juncture in her young life, could Esther get past herself to fully see that truth? King Ahasuerus had offered her a life with little resistance, and lavish, carefree living. God had presented her an opportunity to fulfill significant responsibilities for the sake of God's people. If you could stand in Esther's royal slippers for a moment, could you relate to her dilemma? None of us are royalty, but we find ourselves at the same crossroads of life the moment we realize the cost of serving the Savior.

Mordecai believed that Esther was facing her life's mission. His words have become immortalized: "*Yet who knows whether you have come to the kingdom for such a time as this?*" (Esther 4:14). Let those words remind all of us in the family of God that we're not here on this earth to accrue vacation days, to amass wealth to leave as inheritances, to worship our physical bodies, or to

"And He has made from one blood every nation of men to dwell on all the face of the earth, and has determined their preappointed times and the boundaries of their dwellings, so that they should seek the Lord, in the hope that they might grope for Him and find Him, though He is not far from each one of us."
—Acts 17:26–27

experience life in the fast lane. In those pivotal moments of life when we sense God calling us to reflect His glory, we are living the moments of significance on our journeys.

 Stepping-Stone

Building on the principle in Acts 17:26–27, reflect on these very basic questions about your time and location, considering how God is wielding His plan in your life.

- What generation were you born into, and what are the basic characteristics of your generation?

- How did you get to the place where you are living now? Working now? Worshiping now?

- With whom has your life intersected for your spiritual good? For their spiritual good?

Chariots and Men

Read Esther 5:1–8:17 in your Bible.

Esther had stepped into a fairy tale. The young Jewish orphan girl had been swept out of poverty to be cared for lavishly, she had received a year of pampering and beauty treatments, and suddenly she had found herself crowned as Queen of Persia. She must have felt a deep gratitude as well as an incredible wonder that God had favored her with such grace. How could she deny the mighty movement of God in her life? But now...but now...the scene had turned ugly, and the marble columns that once stood in her palace home as symbols of Esther's great blessings and status had become gray and cold.

Her circumstances changed overnight. Had God also changed? Had His favor been removed?

My toddler son is petrified when we put him on any sort of motorized vehicle. He screams as we near a golf cart or train ride, and we have to force him to board. After the vehicle begins to move and he realizes he's not in danger, he finally relaxes, but we go through this same scenario every time he gets on a ride. I wonder if he'll ever learn to trust a train ride. We adults are not much different, having short memories in the face of adversity or fear. Queen Esther was facing a crisis of oppression of her people, but her deeper problem was a crisis of faith; could she continue to trust God as she tumbled down the mountain of serenity and into the valley of trouble?

In the book of Joshua, God was recounting through Joshua to the Hebrew people what they had experienced since the days of Abraham. As he reached the part of their story concerning their deliverance from Egypt, God said, *"And your eyes saw what I did in Egypt. Then you dwelt in the wilderness a long time"* (Joshua 24:7). What happened? In Egypt God performed unmistakable miracles on a colossal scale that were obviously all in their favor, but they soon forgot God's goodness and His trustworthiness when their bellies growled and their feet grew weary. As a result, these highly favored people of God expired an entire generation by wandering in the wilderness.

"And your eyes saw what I did in Egypt. Then you dwelt in the wilderness a long time."
—Joshua 24:7

In Scripture, the wilderness is a desolate place of despair. We've all had our share of wilderness experiences. The wilderness is that place where we realize we can no longer depend on our husbands, our credit cards, or our great connections to get us out of the crisis that's brought us there. In that desolate place, we come to the end of ourselves and we realize that only mighty God can take us by the hand and lead us out of the wilderness, and then God suddenly has our undivided attention. What will God then say to us? He will speak a calming word, like, *"Peace, be still!"* (Mark 4:39). God says, *"Behold, I will... bring her into the wilderness, and speak comfort to her"* (Hosea 2:14). God would not have us wandering in the wilderness, for as we wander our souls faint while lost people continue to perish. When we're in the wilderness, will we choose to trust God, or will we choose to wander aimlessly?

"Therefore, behold, I will allure her, will bring her into the wilderness, and speak comfort to her."
—Hosea 2:14

Queen Esther called for a three-day fast among her people and expressed her resolve for total abandonment of personal protection: *"If I perish, I perish!"* (Esther 4:16). She turned her face toward God and relinquished to Him complete control over the situation of her people as well as the danger for herself. God is ever faithful, and not only was Esther's life spared, but her people were saved while their enemies perished (Esther 9). There's no better place to rest our trust than in God's hands. *"Some trust in chariots, and some in horses; but we will remember the name of the Lord our God"* (Psalm 20:7).

Dear sisters in Jesus, we can no longer continue to place our personal comfort and protection above the desperate needs of the lost and suffering. We must not think of ourselves; we must think of others. We must not focus on the potential for our loss; we must see the potential for their gain. We must not count on a person or a program for help; *"our help is in the name of the Lord, who made heaven and earth"* (Psalm 124:8). Will you make the choice to abandon self for the sake of helping others in the name of Jesus? Your answer to the question has eternal consequences for others, and highlights the significance of your journey.

 ## Retracing Your Steps to Stay on Course

LIFE LESSON OF ESTHER: Esther chose to abandon her place of comfort and safety for the sake of the lives of others, embracing the divine appointment God had scheduled for her.

I can say with confidence, *"But I am like a green olive tree in the house of God; I trust in the mercy of God forever and ever. I will praise You forever, because You have done it; and in the presence of Your saints I will wait on Your name, for it is good"* (Psalm 55:9).

I am weary of barricading myself from discomfort at the expense of others who are hurting, and I know that my comfort simply is not significant. I want to present my body as a living sacrifice unto God (Romans 12:1). I will no longer be about self-preservation, for I believe that God will preserve me according to His perfect will.

- Instead of being _____, I will be like a healthy, vibrant tree in God's orchard.
- Instead of _____, I will count on God's mercy in every situation.
- Instead of having _____ thoughts, I will praise God in advance for victories in His name.
- Instead of demonstrating _____ in the presence of my brothers and sisters in Christ, I will walk in quiet assurance, believing in God's reliable name as I wait for Him to resolve the situations of my life.

I want to abandon myself for the sake of helping others find Jesus. If I perish, I perish.

SIGNIFICANCE CONNECTION: God is calling believers to abandon their self-made places of comfort and safety to get personally involved in the lives of others, embracing the principle that God intersects believers with unbelievers that the gospel might spread.

God is calling me to get personally involved in the lives of people who are in need. My flesh already wants to put up a barrier, but I will resist that temptation and trust God. I will pray about these people in need of spiritual help who intersect with my life:

I will pray about these people in need of physical help who intersect with my life:

I will pray about serving in or starting the following ministries that intentionally reach out to people in great need:

 ## Stepping Up to the Challenge

Choosing to abandon self-made places of comfort and safety will have a major impact on your closest relationships. Your closest companions in life, such as a husband, son, daughter, mother, father, or friend, will sense this major shift in your life, and they may feel unsure of how to adjust in the relationship. Who will be impacted the most? Write a letter to that person, explaining what God is teaching you about putting others' needs before your own enjoyment, and ask for their support as you learn to make this lifestyle adjustment. If you prefer, sit down in person and have this important talk with the loved ones who can cheer you on as you seize every opportunity "for such a time as this."

How to Become a Christian

God desires to have a personal relationship with you.

For I know the thoughts that I think toward you, says the Lord, thoughts of peace and not of evil, to give you a future and a hope.
—Jeremiah 29:11

But our sin separates us from God. All of us are sinners; no one can live up to God's holy standard, which is perfection.

For all have sinned and come short of the glory of God.
—Romans 3:23

The penalty we deserve for our sin is spiritual death—total separation from God in hell.

For the wages of sin is death, but the gift of God is eternal life in Christ Jesus our Lord.
—Romans 6:23

God is offering you the gift of eternal life through Jesus Christ.

"For God so loved the world that He gave His only begotten Son that whosoever believes in Him should not perish but have everlasting life."
—John 3:16

Jesus Christ is the Son of God. He is the one and only bridge to God.

Jesus said to him, "I am the way, the truth, and the life. No one comes to the Father except through me."
—John 14:6

Jesus lived a sinless life. He allowed Himself to be nailed to the cross to pay the price for our sins so we would not have to face hell. What a wonderful act of love! He died on the cross, was buried, and then rose from the grave.

But God demonstrates His own love toward us, in that while we were still sinners, Christ died for us.
—Romans 5:8

God is offering you new life in Jesus Christ. Do you want to become a Christian? Then go to God in prayer:

1. Admit you are a sinner, asking for forgiveness and turning from your sins.
2. Confess that Jesus, the Son of God, died on the cross and rose again to save you from your sins.
3. Invite Jesus to be the Savior and Lord of your life.

   Dear God, I know that I am a sinner. I am asking for Your forgiveness, and I want to turn away from my sins. I believe that Jesus, Your Son, died on the Cross and rose again to save me from my sins, and I now put my trust in Him as my personal Lord and Savior. Amen.

Whoever calls upon the name of the Lord shall be saved.
—Romans 10:13

If you have prayed to receive Christ, you have been given forgiveness and eternal life!

Group Leader's Guide

What an amazing experience God has in store for you as you guide a group of women along their *Journey to Significance: Becoming Women of Divine Destiny*. May the Lord grant each woman an amazing insight into God's glory reflected in her life as she chooses to walk with Him on her journey to significance.

Bible Study Format Options

You may decide to conduct the study over six weeks or as a weekend retreat. Decide which format best meets the needs of the women you desire to reach.

Six-Week Study

Women will complete one chapter per week for six weeks. At your weekly sessions, the group will discuss their thoughts and reflections from the chapter just completed. One-hour sessions are recommended.

Anything you can do to create an inviting and open atmosphere will bless and encourage each woman to get involved by sharing from her heart during the group discussions. You may decide to begin one week early in order to allow women to meet one another and to introduce the Bible study, kicking off the journey in style. Sunglasses or other traveling gear for the first gathering can add a fun touch. And don't forget, every good journey requires snacks! (Trail mix might be in order.)

Weekend Retreat

A retreat is an ideal setting for women to gain spiritual perspective as they seek to go deeper in their relationships with God. A good mix of large group Bible study and small group discussion time will make the experience "high impact" yet also refreshing and fun.

For a retreat schedule of six one-hour sessions, give an overview of each chapter for the first 40 minutes, allowing the remaining 20 minutes for small group discussion. Based on the material in each chapter that you wish to emphasize, select four or five Stepping Stone questions for small group discussion. You may choose to follow a schedule similar to the following:

Possible Retreat Schedule

Friday
    5:30–6:15 Dinner and Worship Music
    6:15–7:15 Session One
    7:15–7:30 Break
    7:30–8:30 Session Two
    8:30–until Dessert Social

Saturday
    8:00–8:45 Breakfast and Worship Music
    8:45–9:45 Session Three
    9:45–10:00 Snack Break
    10:00–11:00 Session Four
    11:00–12:00 Session Five
    12:00–12:45 Lunch
    12:45–1:45 Session Six
    1:45–2:00 Wrap-Up Discussion and Departure

You may choose to schedule a *Journey to Significance* reunion celebration at six weeks after your retreat. Encourage women to go through each chapter on their own during those six weeks, completing the reading and answering those questions that weren't discussed at the retreat, and allow women to give testimonies during the celebration about what God has taught them about being women of "divine destiny"!

Creating the Greatest Impact

The following elements will help create the greatest impact for each woman taking this journey.

1. Encourage women to pair up as prayer partners during the Bible study. Ask them to be in communication with one another at least once a week outside of group meeting times.

2. Ask women to give one another the gift of open sharing within the group with the agreement of no sharing outside the group. The journey to significance is an exciting yet challenging path, and women may feel a strong need for support through group interaction. Women will desire to share their feelings, reflections, frustrations, and questions with one another, without feeling concerned that their words will be spread outside of the group.

3. The journey to significance is not a road only to be studied; it's a trail to be blazed! From session to session, challenge women to put their studies into practice. Celebrate any steps, whether big or small, that women are taking from week to week on their journeys.

4. Encourage participants to capture the moments of their journey on paper by keeping a journal of experiences and reflections. They will appreciate their efforts by the end of the study, when they have the privilege to look back and reflect on the journey.

5. Make the commitment to yourself and to your group that you will pray for each woman by name daily as she takes this journey to significance.

Session Ideas for Each Chapter

Your group session for each chapter can take any number of formats based on the specific needs of your group. Here are some suggestions for group discussion. (Sentences in quotation marks are questions or comments to read aloud to the group.)

Character Study 1: Joseph, Son of Jacob

Taking the Scenic Route: Building Character Through Perseverance

CONVERSATION STARTERS: (10 MINUTES)

1. "What were your dreams when you were a little girl?"

2. "Joseph's brothers accused him of being a dreamer. Do you take time to dream? To think about your future? To sit still and listen to what God would tell you about your path? Why or why not?"

GETTING INTO THE LESSON: (30 MINUTES)

1. (Read Jeremiah 29:11–13.) "What makes us doubt these words in our daily lives?"

2. (Read James 1:2–4.) Note to the group that we're called not only to endure, but to be joyful in our trials; the trials can be expected to come in any shape or form, including physical, emotional, financial, or other, and there's no promise in the Scripture that the trials will be "fair"; the trials are for God's greater purpose of strengthening our spiritual endurance for the race set before us, and we can stunt our own spiritual growth when we interfere with God's work of building patience in our lives. "What does it mean to allow patience to have 'its perfect work'"?

3. "Joseph's trials in his young life were not only for his benefit and strengthening; part of his divine destiny was the great testimony he gave

at each leg of his journey. What impact do you think Joseph had on the other servants in Potiphar's house? What about Joseph's fellow prisoners?" (Allow women to respond.) "Through Joseph's life, we can see that our challenges in life are not always about us; God is not only doing a work in our own lives, but He often uses our journey to impact the hearts of the people around us.

How is God reaching the people in your sphere of influence as they observe the way you as a Christian are dealing with the struggles and difficulties of your life?"

4. Ask the women to look back at the Stepping Stone on page 21 concerning Psalm 1:1–3. Encourage them to share their responses.

5. "Joseph suffered much hardship because of the malicious or careless acts of others, yet he did not die a bitter man. Joseph learned two valuable life lessons: he learned to prosper under God's authority regardless of his circumstances, and he learned to forgive. Have you had to face either of these life lessons?" (Allow women to respond.) "What did Paul have to say about the trials of his life in Philippians 4:11–13?"

6. Allow women to discuss any Stepping Stone exercise that was particularly meaningful to them.

SUMMARIZING THE SESSION: (20 MINUTES)
Guide the women through a time of sharing their reflections and responses to the closing sections of the chapter (*Retracing Your Steps to Stay on Course*, *Significance Connection*, and *Stepping Up to the Challenge*.) These questions provide an opportunity for each woman to personalize and apply the spiritual emphases of the chapter. Some of their responses may be too personal to discuss with the group; allow women the freedom to share as they feel led. If your group is large, you may choose to break into smaller groups of two or three for this last portion of discussion time, and encourage them to hold one another accountable to allow God to make lasting changes in their lives through their study of this chapter.

Close the session by allowing women to answer the question, "What is the greatest lesson you have learned this week about being a woman of divine destiny?" Have a closing time of prayer, being specific in asking God to help each of you apply the spiritual truths in this chapter. (If you chose to pair women as prayer partners, you may prefer to close with a special prayer time between prayer partners.)

Character Study 2: David

Stepping Out: Finding Courage to Take Action

CONVERSATION STARTERS: (10 MINUTES)

1. "Are you a risk-taker? What is the greatest risk you've ever taken in your life?"
2. "David is famous for battling a giant, armed with nothing but a slingshot. What have been the 'giants' of your life?"

GETTING INTO THE LESSON: (30 MINUTES)

1. (Read 1 Peter 2:9–10.) "Before David could bring glory to God, he had to first accept that he belonged to God as His chosen vessel. Look at the listing in this passage that describes who we are as chosen women of God:
   - Royalty (joint heirs with Jesus Christ, the King)
   - Members of God's priesthood (having direct access to God through the Holy Spirit in our lives, and called to minister to others)
   - A holy nation (a people set apart and distinctly different from the world)
   - God's special people (treasured by Him, peculiar to the world)

   Which of these characteristics bestowed upon us by God means the most to you?" (Allow women to respond.) "According to verse 9, what is God's purpose for us as His chosen people?"

2. (Read Acts 9:10–19.) "Ananias was faced with danger. Just like David, he was not strong enough to overcome the potential danger, but he knew he could trust God. Note in verse 10 that Ananias recognized the voice of God. Knowing that God is directing us gives us courage. How can you know when God is calling you to take a leap of faith?" (Direct the women to John 10:4). "Ananias brought up Saul's reputation and the potential for danger. Why do you suppose God didn't respond to Ananias' concerns by telling him about Saul's conversion?" (Possible answer: God wanted Ananias to trust God and build courage.) "Consider David's great act of courage in the Valley of Elah compared to Ananias' act of courage to visit Saul. How did each man contribute to the kingdom of God? How did their courageous actions strengthen others?"

3. Direct the women to discuss the Stepping Stone on pages 41 in their books.

4. Allow women to discuss any Stepping Stone exercise that was particularly meaningful to them.

SUMMARIZING THE SESSION: (20 MINUTES)

Guide the women through a time of sharing their reflections and responses to the closing sections of the chapter (*Retracing Your Steps to Stay on Course*, *Significance Connection*, and *Stepping Up to the Challenge*.) These questions provide an opportunity for each woman to personalize and apply the spiritual emphases of the chapter. Some of their responses may be too personal to discuss with the group; allow women the freedom to share as they feel led. If your group is large, you may choose to break into smaller groups of two or three for this last portion of discussion time, and encourage them to hold one another accountable to allow God to make lasting changes in their lives through their study of this chapter.

Close the session by allowing women to answer the question, "What is the greatest lesson you have learned this week about being a woman of divine destiny?" Have a closing time of prayer, being specific in asking God to help each of you apply the spiritual truths in this chapter. (If you chose to pair women as prayer partners, you may prefer to close with a special prayer time between prayer partners.)

Character Study 3: Mary of Bethany

Taking Time to Refuel: Intimacy with the Savior

CONVERSATION STARTERS: (10 MINUTES)

1. "The opening question of this chapter asked you to decide if people would likely describe you as efficient, godly, dependable, or busy. Which word did you choose, and why?"
2. "As you studied this week about being a Martha-type versus having a Mary lifestyle, did you think about your own lifestyle and the time you have to commit to being more like Mary (surrendered to the Lord with time and attention)? Do you think most women feel forced to be Martha-types, or is it by choice?"

GETTING INTO THE LESSON: (30 MINUTES)

1. "What do you admire about Martha?" (Allow women to respond.) "According to these verses of Scripture, what is the value of doing good works?" (Direct the women to look up and discuss Matthew 5:16, Colossians 1:10, and 1 Peter 2:12. Encourage the women to see their good works as a means of displaying the glory of Christ before others, pointing them to the Savior.)
2. "As difficult as it may seem for us as busy women to sit still and meditate on

the Word of God, or to devote extra time to prayer, how amazing it is that the God of the universe never struggles to find time for us! Let's look at Psalm 8:3-4." (Read the passage aloud.) "How can we express our gratitude to God for His desire and openness to spend time with us?"

3. (Read Psalm 19:14.) "Is it possible for our words and our mind's thoughts to be different?" (Encourage women to think about the temptation as Christians to have empty words of "Christian talk" when our hearts are angry or distracted.) "God sees what our minds are up to, and He knows what we meditate on – what we think about over and over in our minds. (Allow women to respond.) What one or two words best describe what you tend to mull over in your mind?" (Allow women to respond.) "What do you desire to meditate on, honoring God and worshiping Him with your mind?" (Allow women to respond.) "What does Malachi 3:16 teach us about our thoughts about God?" (Possible answer: The people talked together about God, stirring up thoughts of God in their minds; God took note of their meditations on Him, and He was pleased.)

4. (Read 2 Corinthians 10:5 from different versions of the Bible.) "We can be proactive about our thoughts, whether it's focusing on God's voice during our Bible study and prayer time each day, or hearing His voice as we go about the activities of our days. How would you like to respond to 2 Corinthians 10:5?" (Allow women to respond.) Encourage women to be aware of their thoughts over the next week. Challenge them to ask God for help in submitting their minds fully during their prayer and Bible study times, and to report next week if they felt more in tune to the Holy Spirit from taking their thoughts "captive" for Christ.

5. (Read 2 Corinthians 2:14-15.) "Our nearness to Christ can make our witness before others more appealing. Has there been a person in your life who had such a strong 'fragrance of Christ' that you felt compelled to draw nearer to God?"

6. Allow women to discuss any Stepping Stone exercise that was particularly meaningful to them.

Summarizing the Session: (20 minutes)
Guide the women through a time of sharing their reflections and responses to the closing sections of the chapter (*Retracing Your Steps to Stay on Course, Significance Connection,* and *Stepping Up to the Challenge.*) These questions provide an opportunity for each woman to personalize and apply the spiritual emphases of the chapter. Some of their responses may be too personal to

discuss with the group; allow women the freedom to share as they feel led. If your group is large, you may choose to break into smaller groups of two or three for this last portion of discussion time, and encourage them to hold one another accountable to allow God to make lasting changes in their lives through their study of this chapter.

Close the session by allowing women to answer the question, "What is the greatest lesson you have learned this week about being a woman of divine destiny?" Have a closing time of prayer, being specific in asking God to help each of you apply the spiritual truths in this chapter. (If you chose to pair women as prayer partners, you may prefer to close with a special prayer time between prayer partners.)

Character Study 4: Daniel
When They Lose Your Luggage: A Commitment to Godliness
CONVERSATION STARTERS: (10 MINUTES)
1. "Can you think of a time when you stepped into a new situation and felt totally unprepared?" (Encourage the women to share about being prepared/ unprepared for marriage, having children, new jobs, helping aging parents, etc.)
2. "Of all of the ways to go about getting spiritually prepared for the various challenges of living a life of divine destiny, which one method do you find most fulfilling?" (Some possible answers that women may discuss are church attendance, women's Bible studies, spiritual retreats, fasting, reading through the Bible each year, daily devotionals, a mentoring relationship with a mature Christian, etc.)

GETTING INTO THE LESSON: (30 MINUTES)
1. "Daniel's life is an incredible testimony of what one man can do under the complete authority of God, and his incredible journey began well: 'But Daniel purposed in his heart that he would not defile himself' (Daniel 1:8). According to Paul, the resolve of mankind to stay undefiled in honor of God is a fading concept as this world begins to near its end." (Read 2 Timothy 3:1–5). "Look through verses 2–4. Can you think of examples of moral decay that match any of Paul's descriptions?" (Allow women to share. Encourage them to think not only of the moral corruption of the world, but also their own personal struggles for holiness as Christians.) "Verse 5 is critical to our study of the life of Daniel, and for our understanding of our

journey to significance. As women of divine destiny, we need God's power in our lives! How do we deny God's power through worldly behavior?" (Possible answer: we hinder the work of the Holy Spirit, our source of power as Christians, when we live for ourselves instead of living for and loving God above all.)

2. "You've heard the phrase 'product of his environment.' How much do you suppose culture has influenced your walk with Christ?" (Allow women to respond.) "According to Leviticus 18:1–4, what does God have to say about the influence of culture and learned behavior as a follower of Christ?" (As women discuss their ideas, emphasize the final words of God in verse 4: God is the Mighty One, and He has the authority to reign in our lives.)

3. "God called upon Daniel to face powerful men with the truth of Holy God. He is calling upon each of us as the ambassadors of Christ to share the gospel truth with others." (Direct the women to read aloud Jeremiah 1:4–10.) "How do God's words encourage you? Can you relate to Jeremiah with his excuses? Look at verse 10 carefully and consider how it relates to tearing down false arguments against Christ in order to plant truth in the hearts of people who need Jesus. Can you trust God with your relationships with unbelievers, allowing some 'tearing down and rooting out' to take place so that 'building and planting' can follow?" (Allow women time to respond to each question.)

4. Direct women to discuss their answers to the Stepping Stone on page 89.

5. Allow women to discuss any Stepping Stone exercise that was particularly meaningful to them.

Summarizing the Session: (20 minutes)

Guide the women through a time of sharing their reflections and responses to the closing sections of the chapter (*Retracing Your Steps to Stay on Course, Significance Connection,* and *Stepping Up to the Challenge.*) These questions provide an opportunity for each woman to personalize and apply the spiritual emphases of the chapter. Some of their responses may be too personal to discuss with the group; allow women the freedom to share as they feel led. If your group is large, you may choose to break into smaller groups of two or three for this last portion of discussion time, and encourage them to hold one another accountable to allow God to make lasting changes in their lives through their study of this chapter.

Close the session by allowing women to answer the question, "What is the greatest lesson you have learned this week about being a woman of divine destiny?" Have a closing time of prayer, being specific in asking God to help each of you apply the spiritual truths in this chapter. (If you chose to pair women as prayer partners, you may prefer to close with a special prayer time between prayer partners.)

Character Study 5: Mary, Mother of Jesus
View From the Backseat: Glorifying Jesus
CONVERSATION STARTERS: (10 MINUTES)

1. "Do you love to be in the spotlight, or do you prefer to be behind the scenes? If you had to perform some task on live television, what would you pick to do, and why?"
2. "Who or what is the biggest competition in your life for the top spot of your heart, or of your daily schedule?" (Possible answers: children who want to be the center of attention, a demanding work schedule, a time-consuming health problem, a full email box, etc.)

GETTING INTO THE LESSON: (30 MINUTES)

1. (Read Isaiah 66:1–2.) "How does God's concept of granting favor differ from the world's methods of dolling out privileges?" (Possible answer: the world often rewards people who climb their way to the top, or who stand out in the crowd for achievement.)
2. "God is worthy to be exalted. He is worthy to receive all of the glory and adoration, and He is worthy of our humble service." (Invite the women to take turns reading aloud passages that proclaim the holiness and glory of God, including Exodus 15:11, Psalm 99:9, Isaiah 6:3, Revelation 15:4, Deuteronomy 32:4, Psalm 18:30, and Ecclesiastes 3:14.) "In view of who God is, how do you better understand who you are as His creation?" (Relate the responses back to Isaiah's response in Isaiah 6:5, and God's blessing upon Isaiah in 6:6–8.)
3. "Mary spent her entire adult life on a huge learning curve, trying to figure out who she was and what her role was to be in relation to Jesus Christ, her Savior as well as her child! Are you currently trying to figure out God's plan for your life? What questions are you asking? Are you ready to say to God, '"Let it be to me"' (Luke 1:38*b*)?"
4. "What new perspectives did you gain as you studied this week about the challenges and humble nature of Mary's assignment as a woman of divine destiny?"

5. (Read Matthew 11:28–30.) "Is Jesus offering to remove the burdens of life for anyone willing to serve Him?" (No) "What is He offering to us?" (Possible answers: He offers to lighten our loads by the helping strength of His mighty hand; He offers to give us satisfaction and rest in our souls as we follow His leadership in our lives; He offers to be our perfect model of humble service to the Father.)
6. Allow women to discuss any Stepping Stone exercise that was particularly meaningful to them.

SUMMARIZING THE SESSION: (20 MINUTES)
Guide the women through a time of sharing their reflections and responses to the closing sections of the chapter (*Retracing Your Steps to Stay on Course*, *Significance Connection*, and *Stepping Up to the Challenge*.) These questions provide an opportunity for each woman to personalize and apply the spiritual emphases of the chapter. Some of their responses may be too personal to discuss with the group; allow women the freedom to share as they feel led. If your group is large, you may choose to break into smaller groups of two or three for this last portion of discussion time, and encourage them to hold one another accountable to allow God to make lasting changes in their lives through their study of this chapter.

Close the session by allowing women to answer the question, "What is the greatest lesson you have learned this week about being a woman of divine destiny?" Have a closing time of prayer, being specific in asking God to help each of you apply the spiritual truths in this chapter. (If you chose to pair women as prayer partners, you may prefer to close with a special prayer time between prayer partners.)

Character Study 6: Esther
No Time to Sightsee: Having an Impact on Your World
CONVERSATION STARTERS: (10 MINUTES)
1. "If you could be queen for a day, how would you spend those 24 hours?"
2. "Esther and the other women received 12 months of beauty treatments —please! If you could receive a little help in the beauty department, what would you take for your 12 months' beauty plan? For what area of inner beauty would you like to receive God's 12-month treatment plan?"

GETTING INTO THE LESSON: (30 MINUTES)

1. "Esther was a woman well-suited and hand-picked by God for this specific role as a woman of divine destiny. Now that you have completed this Bible study, *Journey to Significance*, what can you share that God has revealed to you about what He has fashioned you to do in your life for His glory?"

2. "Whatever God's calling is in your life, He will direct you to have an impact for the kingdom of God by reaching people for Christ. Sharing Jesus with others takes patience, courage, and the love of Christ, and certainly you can expect to get involved in a personal way." (Direct women to share their responses to the Stepping Stone questions on pages 133.) 3. "How fitting for us to consider Queen Esther as our last study on this *Journey to Significance*, for she had the means of living a life of luxury for herself, just as we might be tempted to miss our divine destiny by focusing on ourselves instead of God's appointed moments to serve Him: "'for such a time as this'" (Esther 4:14b)." (Read Luke 10:30–37.) "Jesus teaches us the same lesson through His story about the actions of not a queen, but a despised common man, a Samaritan, in this parable. What possible excuses could the priest and Levite have offered for why they chose not to get involved to help the wounded man?" (Encourage women to realize that the priest and Levite missed their opportunity of "divine destiny," making their religion of little use to the hurting man; relate this principle to the women's opportunities to minister to the hurting of this world, a truly high calling significant to the kingdom of God.) "What was the price paid by the Samaritan to help the wounded man?" (Possible answers: He gave of his wages, which may have been a great sacrifice for him; he walked instead of riding into town because he gave up his transportation; he placed himself in possible danger; he set himself up for the potential of being verbally abused by the very man he saved, because Jews generally hated Samaritans; he gave up a great deal of time to help this man, and would have had to return to the inn a second time; he went to great lengths to help a man, though he would probably not be publicly honored or thanked.)

4. (Read Philippians 1:20–21 and Galatians 2:20.) "What is divine destiny? What is significant in the eyes of God?"

5. Allow women to discuss any Stepping Stone exercise that was particularly meaningful to them.

SUMMARIZING THE SESSION: (20 MINUTES)

Guide the women through a time of sharing their reflections and responses to the closing sections of the chapter (Retracing Your Steps to Stay on Course, Significance Connection, and Stepping Up to the Challenge.) These questions provide an opportunity for each woman to personalize and apply the spiritual emphases of the chapter. Some of their responses may be too personal to discuss with the group; allow women the freedom to share as they feel led. If your group is large, you may choose to break into smaller groups of two or three for this last portion of discussion time, and encourage them to hold one another accountable to allow God to make lasting changes in their lives through their study of this chapter.

Close the session by allowing women to answer the question, "What is the greatest lesson you have learned this week about being a woman of divine destiny?" Have a closing time of prayer, being specific in asking God to help each of you apply the spiritual truths in this chapter. (If you chose to pair women as prayer partners, you may prefer to close with a special prayer time between prayer partners.)

Kimberly is available to lead *Journey to Significance* women's retreats. She can be contacted through her Web site, www.KimberlySowell.com.

New Hope® Publishers is a division of WMU®,
an international organization that challenges Christian believers
to understand and be radically involved in God's mission.
For more information about WMU, go to www.wmu.com.
More information about New Hope books may be found
at www.newhopepublishers.com. New Hope books
may be purchased at your local bookstore.

MORE SMALL-GROUP
BIBLE STUDIES FOR

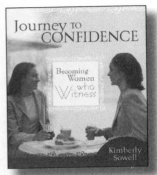

Journey to Confidence
Becoming Women Who Witness
Kimberly Sowell
ISBN: 1-56309-923-3

Pull Up a Chair
You, Me, and the Gospel of John
Lorie Looney Keene
ISBN: 1-59669-202-2

Before His Throne
*Discovering the Wonder of
Intimacy with a Holy God*
Kathy Howard
ISBN: 1-59669-201-4

Refresh
Sharing Stories. Building Faith.
Kathy Escobar and Laura Greiner
ISBN: 1-59669-069-0

Available in bookstores everywhere

For information about these books or any New Hope product, visit www.newhopepublishers.com